THE COLLECTED  L

VOLUME VIII

SPIRITS
HOLY AND UNHOLY

JACK COTTRELL

THE CHRISTIAN RESTORATION ASSOCIATION

TABLE OF CONTENTS

PREFACE

For the first time in this series of collected works, I am having to combine two subjects into one volume. I wanted to have enough material on the Holy Spirit to fill a book, but it did not happen. So, after pondering the possibilities, I decided this would make an interesting combination: the Holy Spirit, and demonic spirits! Adding the latter category was just right to fill out my allotted space. Besides, it seemed appropriate since the word "spirit" occurs in both, which lends itself to a good title: *Spirits: Holy and Unholy*. (I usually am a bit more logical than that, though.)

As I think about it, I cannot remember ever having a Bible College or seminary course on either of these subjects. I cannot remember that such a course was offered in any school I attended. Thinking here first about the *Holy* Spirit, He did not find His way into any of their course offerings. Christology, yes; the Holy Spirit, no. This is probably because, even in the Bible, the Spirit has a more subdued role in the salvation drama than does Jesus the Redeemer. This may be why Frederick Dale Bruner and William Hordern titled a book they published in 2001 as *The Holy Spirit: Shy Member of the Trinity*. Then in 2009 Francis Chan wrote one called *Forgotten God: Reversing Our Tragic Neglect of the Holy Spirit*.

Not I, Lord! Once my teaching career got under way, sticking a course on the Holy Spirit into our seminary curriculum was a no-brainer. I was able to do this because I was in charge of the theology department at our school. The Bible College I attended (Cincinnati Bible Seminary— yes, it was a college) did not have a separate graduate school until 1956.

Within a few years the dean, Dr. Lewis Foster, began to build a separate graduate faculty. Around 1960 he asked me if I would be interested in becoming the first full-time theology professor for the CBS graduate school! I said yes. One result was that I was able to develop the theology department and curriculum from scratch. Thus I was able to begin offering a course on the Holy Spirit from the beginning of my tenure in 1967. (I was the only theology professor for around twenty years. Over my forty-eight years of teaching there, I developed and taught over forty courses.)

Anyway, once I began teaching on the Holy Spirit, my interest in the subject grew. I began to see how important the work of the Spirit is in our lives as Christians. Also, it became obvious to me that many of the doctrines that divide Christians involve false views of the Holy Spirit. So I continued to delve into the Biblical teaching on the person and work of the Spirit. In 2007 I was able to publish a book, summing up my understanding of the subject: *Power from on High: What the Bible Says About the Holy Spirit* (College Press). It is over 500 pages long. (See also my shorter study, *The Holy Spirit: A Biblical Study*, 131 pp., published by College Press in 2006.)

Along the way I have also spoken much on the Holy Spirit in local churches, and occasionally written for publication short pieces on various aspects of this topic. Many of the oral presentations and most of the written pieces are included in this volume. At the very beginning is a series of talks that I was invited to give for the Michigan Christian Convention in 2012. The suggested theme was "God's Power in You—the Holy Spirit." You can see how I developed that theme in Section One of this book. This is the first time they have been published; study them carefully!

Section Two has twelve miscellaneous studies on various aspects of the Spirit's person and work, many of which were written in answer to questions from my Facebook friends. These are the shorter ones. I would especially recommend a couple of the longer ones. One is called "The Promise of the Father." I wrote this one just a few weeks ago, for presentation at the Christian Restoration Association's 2018 Bible

Conference held in October. Another one I would emphasize is "Does the Holy Spirit Give Miraculous Gifts Today? A Study of 1 Corinthians 13:8-13." (For much more detail on such subjects, see my book.)

The last section is on a different kind of spiritual being—not "Holy Spirit," but *evil spirits*. This latter is one of the Biblical names for demons. Somewhere along the way in my teaching career I came to realize that we really needed a course on this subject at CBS. Until the early 1970s I had not given much thought to this subject; I had been taught that demons are not active today. So why worry about them? Then in the early 70s we were hit with a serious cultural change: the occult came out of the closet. Witchcraft, sorcery, spiritism, and all sorts of sinister practices became "respectable" and acceptable in our relativist culture. Many books were being published on the subject, both pro and con. In reading such material I came to see that I and many others had been deceived: demons are very active in our world today. For many years thereafter I taught one-credit courses on both the occult and demonology.

I never wrote a lot about either of these subjects, though. Maybe someday I can write up my lecture notes for a small book. Until then, here are a few pieces that might point you in the right direction on how to think about demons. (I have some material on the occult itself that I hope to publish in a later volume in this series, possibly with some pieces on cults. Look for it: Cults and the Occult.)

As usual, all Scripture references are from the NASB and the ESV, unless noted otherwise.

JACK COTTRELL
September 13, 2018

SECTION ONE

MICHIGAN CHRISTIAN CONVENTION 2012:

MESSAGES ON THE WORK OF THE HOLY SPIRIT

OVERVIEW

In 2012 I was privileged to be asked to be the main speaker for the Michigan Christian Convention, which involved presenting five messages or lessons on the works of the Holy Spirit. Below are short descriptions of my five sessions, followed by the full text of those lessons.

1. **The Bible View vs. Liberalism.** The most important thing the Holy Spirit ever did for us is *give us the Bible*, through His work of inspiration. As has happened many times in the past, the church is once again being challenged by subtle attacks on the Bible's authority. Such attacks are in effect attacks upon the Holy Spirit, and must be confronted seriously and vigorously.

2. **The Bible View vs. Calvinism.** In the New Covenant era a major work of the Holy Spirit is the saving act of *regeneration*, performed upon the heart of the submitting sinner. Calvinism has distorted this teaching into the false doctrine of irresistible grace; many Restorationists have overreacted to the Calvinist view and have denied actual regeneration altogether. Here we will examine what the Bible says on the subject.

3. **The Bible View vs. Pentecostalism.** A major aspect of the Holy Spirit's work is to bestow upon individuals certain abilities and

ministries that will enable them to meet the needs of the body of believers as a whole. In the early decades of the church some of these gifts were supernatural or miraculous in nature. Here we will examine and critique the claims of Pentecostals and Charismatics, that such gifts still exist today.

4. **The Bible View vs. Mysticism.** Following baptism, the Holy Spirit continues to dwell personally in the life of every believer. However, many Christians do not understand the purpose of the Spirit's indwelling. Many think He is within us to give us some kind of mystical "guidance." Here we will see that His purpose is to give us *sanctifying* power—the power to be holy, and not to give us mystical or subjective knowledge of any sort.

5. **The Eight-fold Path to Holiness.** The previous lesson emphasized the *fact* that the Holy Spirit dwells within us for the purpose of giving us the power to overcome sin and lead holy lives. This lesson follows up on this theme by suggesting eight practical steps that Christians should follow as the means of accessing the power of the Holy Spirit within us. This is the "how to" aspect of the general theme.

PART ONE:
THE BIBLE VS. LIBERALISM

INTRODUCTION

We know there IS a "Holy Spirit." We use the baptismal formula of Matthew 28:18-20; we sing the doxology: "Praise Father, Son, and Holy Ghost!" We know He is a DIVINE PERSON: He is part of the Trinity, equal with the Father and the Son. We know He WORKS in the world – but here we get a little fuzzy in our thinking. Exactly what does the Holy Spirit do? This is what we want to explore in these lessons.

I.   GENERAL THOUGHTS ON THE WORK OF THE HOLY SPIRIT

When theologians talk about the Trinity, they usually distinguish between the *ontological* Trinity and the *economic* Trinity. The former term applies to the nature or essence of the Trinity as the three persons exist within themselves and relate to each other. The latter term applies when we are thinking about the *workings* of these three persons, and when we recognize that each person of the Trinity has distinct and unique tasks, especially in relation to the works of redemption.

This is definitely true of the Holy Spirit. Throughout the Old and New Testaments we see that the Holy Spirit is carrying out distinctive activities among the people of God. He is actually quite busy—busier than we may think. As we analyze the records of the Spirit's works, we see that He bestows upon us various kinds of *gifts*—four in particular. He gives us *truth* gifts, *sign* gifts, *service* gifts, and *salvation* gifts. These are divided into two main categories: (1) gifts of KNOWLEDGE, which include the truth gifts; and (2) gifts of POWER, which include the sign, service, and salvation gifts.

The gifts of power are as follows. The sign gifts give us *miraculous* power; the service gifts give us *ministering* power; and the salvation gifts give us *moral* power. It is very important to understand how these gifts are distinguished. They are not all given all the time. Failure to understand this has been a source of great misunderstanding.

This particular lesson explores the truth gifts: it explains how the Holy Spirit gives us *knowledge*. This has also been seriously misunderstood.

When I first started speaking on this subject in churches and Christian groups, I always began with this lesson: "Who Is the Holy Spirit, and What Is the Most Important Thing He Ever Did for Us?" Regarding the question in the second part of this lesson, the answer was always this: The most important thing the Holy Spirit ever did for us is that HE GAVE US THE BIBLE. The Dutch theologian Abraham Kuyper put it this way: "Among the divine works of art produced by the Holy Spirit, the Sacred Scripture stands first. It may seem incredible that the printed pages of a book should excel His spiritual work in human hearts, yet we assign to the Sacred Scripture the most conspicuous place without hesitation" (*The Work of the Holy Spirit*, tr. H. de Vries [Eerdmans, 1966], p. 56).

II. WHAT THE BIBLE TEACHES ABOUT THE SPIRIT'S ROLE IN GIVING US THE BIBLE

Here is one of the most mind-boggling thoughts you can imagine: **God wants to communicate with us!** God wants to transfer ideas from

HIS mind to ours! He does not do this directly to each individual; He does it through go-betweens or mediators called *prophets*. He gives messages to them to be passed along to the rest of us. Here is a major work of the Holy Spirit: the truth gift of *revelation*. But how can God be sure the prophets will get it right when they pass these messages along to the rest of us? Here is where the Holy Spirit enters the process again, through what we call *inspiration*. These two actions—revelation and inspiration—are the TRUTH gifts given to selected individuals in Bible days. The following are some key Biblical passages on this work of the Spirit (from the NASB):

- **2 Samuel 23:2** (among the last words of David) – "The Spirit of the LORD spoke by me, and His word was on my tongue."

- **Acts 1:16** (the Apostle Peter speaking) – "Brethren, the Scripture had to be fulfilled, which the Holy Spirit foretold by the mouth of David concerning Judas."

- **Acts 28:25** (the Apostle Paul speaking to Jewish leaders in Rome) – "The Holy Spirit rightly spoke through Isaiah the prophet to your fathers."

- **2 Peter 1:21** – "For no prophecy was ever made by an act of human will, but men moved by the Holy Spirit spoke from God."

- **John 16:12-13** (Jesus speaking to the Apostles) – "I have many more things to say to you, but you cannot bear them now. But when He, the Spirit of truth, comes, He will guide you into all the truth."

- **1 Corinthians 2:9-13** ("we" and "us" refer specifically to apostles and prophets) – "But just as it is written, 'Things which eye has not seen and ear has not heard, and which have not entered the heart of man, all that God has prepared for those who love Him.' For to us God revealed them through the Spirit; for the Spirit searches all things, even the depths of God. For who among men knows the thoughts of a man except the spirit of the man which is in him? Even so the thoughts of God no one knows except the Spirit of God. Now we have received, not the spirit of the world, but the Spirit who is from God, so that we may know the things freely given to us by God, which things we also speak, not in words taught by human wisdom, but in those taught by the Spirit, combining spiritual thoughts with spiritual words."

- **Ephesians 3:5** (speaking again of the "mystery of Christ") – "which in other generations was not made known to the sons of men, as it has now been revealed to His holy apostles and prophets in the Spirit."

- **1 Peter 1:10-12** – "As to this salvation, the prophets who prophesied of the grace that would come to you made careful searches and inquiries, seeking to know what person or time the Spirit of Christ within them was indicating as He predicted the sufferings of Christ and the glories to follow. It was revealed to them that they were not serving themselves, but you, in these things which now have been announced to you through those who preached the gospel to you by the Holy Spirit sent from heaven—things into which angels long to look."

Just how important is this? Because of this work of the Holy Spirit, the BIBLE—the book that we use every day and take for granted most of the time—is in truth *the very words of God* in our own human language! Speaking of the Old Testament Scriptures, Paul says that the Jews were greatly privileged because they were entrusted with *ta logia tou theou* – "the very words of God" (Romans 3:2, NIV). In 1 Thessalonians 2:13-15 Paul says his own teaching is the "Word of God," and that this is so whether it was his oral or written teaching. He could say this because he knew that he was speaking and writing through "the Spirit of God" (1 Corinthians 7:40).

Citing Deuteronomy 8:3, Jesus responded to a satanic temptation with these words: "Man shall not live by bread alone, but by every word that comes from the mouth of God" (Matthew 4:4). In discussing the Old Testament's teaching, Jesus calls it "the commandment of God" and "the Word of God" (Mark 7:8, 13). No wonder He can cite a rather obscure Scripture (Psalms 82:6) in a debate with the Jewish leaders and decisively affirm, "And the Scriptures cannot be broken" (John 10:35).

Why is it important that the Bible is the WORD OF GOD? Because of its content! Think about all the deep questions of life with which philosophers and theologians have wrestled for millennia: Is there a God? What is He like? Is He friendly toward us? Where did the universe/life/man come from? Is there such a thing as right vs. wrong? Does human existence have a purpose? Do I need salvation? If so, what is it, and how is it accomplished? Is there life after death? Is there a judgment day?

Here is the remarkable thing: All of these questions are answered in the Holy Spirit-inspired BIBLE! What if someone does not know about the Bible, or does not accept the Bible as God's Word? Just think about how human beings have struggled to try to answer these crucial questions without the Bible! But for us who know and believe the Bible, we have the answers—the answers to life's most important questions in permanent, objective form! What could be more significant than this? Here is the point: the fact that we have these answers is the result of the Holy Spirit's work of revelation and inspiration! Can we doubt that this is the most important thing the Holy Spirit ever did for us?

Because it is the Spirit-inspired Word of God, the Bible plays a fundamental role in our lives. This is true of the life of the church as such. In Ephesians 2:20 Paul says that the church is "built on the foundation of the apostles and prophets, Christ Jesus Himself being the corner stone."

From its very beginning the church has devoted itself to "the apostles' teaching" (Acts 2:42).

The Bible is also indispensable in our lives individually. John 20:30-31 reminds us of this importance: "Therefore many other signs Jesus also performed in the presence of the disciples, which are not written in this book; but these have been written so that you may believe that Jesus is the Christ, the Son of God, and that believing you may have life in His name." Romans 1:16 adds: "For I am not ashamed of the gospel, for it is the power of God for salvation to everyone who believes." Also, 2 Timothy 3:15-17 cannot be over-emphasized: "The sacred writings ... are able to make you wise for salvation through faith in Christ Jesus. All Scripture is breathed out by God and profitable for teaching, for reproof, for correction, and for training in righteousness, that the man of God may be competent, equipped for every good work" (ESV). See Hebrews 4:12.

This is why we say: "Sola Scriptura!" and "The Bible, and the Bible alone, is our only infallible rule of faith and practice!"

III. THE CHALLENGE OF LIBERALISM

What is liberalism? In a theological context, it refers to any individual or group that denies the full and absolute truth of the Bible. In other words, it is the denial of the inerrancy of Scripture. (There are differing degrees of liberalism; some versions are more radical than others.)

The inevitable result of such a denial is that *something else* is substituted for the authority of the Bible, and that "something else" becomes our "rule of faith and practice." Often the "something else" is some *part* of the Bible or something *within* the Bible, a "canon within the canon." Most often, at least at first, *Jesus Himself* becomes the source and test for all sound teaching. I call this the Christological fallacy, and it is fallacious (wrong) on many levels. Others say that only the "faith and practice" (i.e., doctrinal) sections of the Bible are inerrant.

When one begins to narrow down the scope of what is inspired and therefore authoritative, ultimately the substitute source and norm for sound doctrine will become *human experience*. This is the case in two ways. First, the new authority takes the form of the *collective* experience of the "church" – i.e., changes in the "christian" world's understanding of "God's will" and "God's purposes" that happen through the absorbing of cultural trends made popular by secular education and secular media, and through the elevation of humanistic values defined solely by love and social justice. Such changes are made on an individual level and on the congregational level under the influence of the spirit of autonomy rather than authority, as determined by relativism rather than absolute truth, and in pursuit of entertainment rather than solemn worship.

And here is the deal: these changes are accepted as a "new work of the Spirit" among us; they are seen as "where the Holy Spirit is leading His church today." The collective experience of Christendom takes the place of the Bible as the only rule of faith and practice, and is attributed to the work of the Holy Spirit. Here I will cite some examples of the kind of thing I am talking about.

Several such examples come from the context of the increasing influence of feminism on the church. One example is from the book by Letha Scanzoni & Nancy Hardesty, in the 1992 edition of their work, *All We're Meant to Be*. As they survey the growing influence of feminist thinking on the churches of America, they make this comment: "Many of us see the wind of the Spirit blowing in these exciting events" (p. 338). Val Webb is another such example. In her book, *Why We're Equal: Introducing Feminist Theology* (Chalice Press, 1999), she surveys the main women in liberal Christian feminism. Their message is that the Bible is a male-oriented book that suppresses and oppresses women. They see their task, however, as rescuing women from such Bible-based oppression and injustice. They see the success of feminist ideology as the work of the Holy

Spirit: "God the Spirit is at work wherever people, including women, struggle for justice" (p. 108).

Letty Russell, a leading liberal feminist theologian, tells about how feminism has taught us that "women's experience," rather than the Bible, "is normative." Feminism has thus liberated the Bible from its "patriarchal worldview" by separating the "Word of God" from the Biblical texts. Because of feminism, people are hearing this Word of God in a totally new way. "This [new] hearing is a gift of the Holy Spirit" (from a book she edited called *Feminist Interpretation of the Bible* [Westminister 1985], pp. 17, 29). Nevertheless, says Russell, there is still a "message of liberation for women" in the Bible, which means we can still use it to restore "wholeness, peace, and justice in the world." When we do this, we can see "the power of the Spirit at work in communities of struggle and faith" (p. 138).

Another example of how collective experience is replacing Biblical authority comes from within the homosexual culture of our time. The following are excerpts from Luke Timothy Johnson's article, "Homosexuality & the Church," in the online magazine *Commonweal*, accessed March 16, 2011, from http://commonwealmagazine.org/print/4188 . In the article Johnson explains how God, or more specifically "God's Holy Spirit," is active in the church today, giving us a new perspective on homosexuality. He says up front that he rejects the teaching of the Bible passages that clearly condemn homosexual activity. "I think it important to state clearly that we do, in fact, reject the straightforward commands of Scripture, and appeal instead to another authority when we declare that same-sex unions can be holy and good. And what exactly is that authority? We appeal explicitly to the weight of our own experience." "Implicit in an appeal to experience is also an appeal to the living God whose creative work never ceases, who continues to shape humans in his image every day, in ways that can surprise and even shock us…. God *does* create the world anew at every moment."

According to Johnson, we "place our trust in the power of the living God to reveal as powerfully through personal experience and testimony as through written texts. To justify this trust, we invoke the basic Pauline principle that the Spirit gives life but the letter kills (2 Corinthians 3:6). And if the letter of Scripture cannot find room for the activity of the living God in the transformation of human lives, then trust and obedience must be paid to the living God rather than to the words of Scripture."

Johnson continues: "What I find most important of all is not the authority found in specific commands, which are fallible, conflicting, and often culturally conditioned, but rather the way Scripture creates the mind of Christ in its readers, authorizing them to reinterpret written texts in light of God's Holy Spirit active in human lives." "If it is risky to trust ourselves to the evidence of God at work in transformed lives even when it challenges the clear statements of Scripture, it is a far greater risk to allow the words of Scripture to blind us to the presence and power of the living God."

In addition to the *collective* experience explained above, the second way that experience is replacing inspired Scripture as the norm for Christian doctrine and Christian living is through *personal* experience, i.e., the subjective judgment of the individual, understood as "guidance" from the Holy Spirit. In the early fifth century A.D., Augustine warned us against this tendency when he said, "If you believe what you like in the gospel, and reject what you don't like, it is not the gospel you believe, but yourself." Substitute "Bible" for "gospel" and it comes out thus: "If you believe what you like in the Bible, and reject what you don't like, it is not the Bible you believe, but yourself."

This appeal to personal experience can take many forms. In the mid-twentieth century, Neo-orthodoxy made it popular to acknowledge a personal "encounter with Christ" as one's starting point for Christian "truth." Others appeal to "the witness of the Holy Spirit" to validate their liberal thinking. An example of this is Stephen T. Davis, in his book, *The*

Debate About the Bible: Inerrancy Versus Infallibility (Westminster 1977). He claims we cannot accept the Bible as *inerrant*, but we can think of it as "infallible." The following are quotations from Davis, with significant selections highlighted:

To claim that the Bible is inerrant is to say that it "contains *no errors at all*," e.g., in history, logic, and geography. But that claim "is one that in all humility I cannot affirm," says Davis (16). **"I consider myself an evangelical Christian and yet I do not affirm inerrancy"** (18). Instead, he believes the Bible is "infallible," i.e., "entirely trustworthy on matters of faith and practice" (16).

Later he qualifies this by limiting infallibility only to "matters that are *crucially relevant* to Christian faith and practice" (118, italics added). But in the end this means nothing, since he says, "I admit that I am unable to stipulate a clear and infallible criterion to distinguish Biblical passages that are crucially relevant to faith and practice from those that are not" (125).

But even if he could do so, it would not make any real difference, since he clearly says that his "faith and practice" distinction "does not necessarily mean that I find no *theological error* in the Bible as opposed, say, to scientific or historical error" (125).

In fact, Davis says, it is always possible that the Bible contains errors in any of its claims; the deal is that he has simply *not found any yet* in matters (crucially relevant) to faith and practice. "There are historical and scientific errors in the Bible, but I have found none on matters of faith and practice. I do not claim *a priori* that the Bible is or must be infallible, just that I have found it to be so. Perhaps someday it will be shown that the Bible is not infallible" (115-116). "I am open at any point to the possibility that the Bible is not infallible" (120).

What criteria shall we apply to determine if any given Biblical doctrine is indeed erroneous? His answer seems to be: human reason, i.e., an examination of the available evidence. "The only epistemological credentials a doctrine must have in order to be accepted by evangelicals is that it seem true on the available evidence." **An evangelical accepts "evangelical doctrines ... simply because they seem true to him."** "I believe B, C, and D because I believe they are taught in the Bible and because I know of no argument or evidence that refutes them." **No Christian can accept a doctrine on the basis of the Bible alone. "He must hold to some other authority or criterion as well. That authority, I am not embarrassed to say, is his own mind, his own ability to reason"** (71). **A Christian must "accept *whatever* the Bible says on *any subject whatsoever* unless there is compelling reason not to accept it. That is, everything in the Bible is authoritative and normative for the Christian until he comes across a passage which for good reasons he cannot accept.... One should reject something that the Bible says only where, having thoroughly examined the problem, in all humility one cannot accept what it says"** (75). "I believe that the Bible is or ought to be authoritative for every Christian in all that it says on any subject unless and until he encounters a passage which after careful study and for good reasons he cannot accept" (116).

Despite this ultimate appeal and apparent dependence on the evidential use of reason, Davis acknowledges "that sin has corrupted all aspects of human personality, including reason, and that reason is not therefore an infallible guide to truth." But this does not change anything: "Corrupted or not, we have no choice but to listen to and follow the dictates of reason" (72).

Where does this leave Davis regarding his use of the Bible for deciding matters of faith and practice? It leaves him in the bottomless and shoreless sea of doctrinal subjectivity and relativity. To change the metaphor, his feet are "firmly planted in mid-air." He labors on, "despite his clear belief that a discovered error on a revelational matter makes the whole Bible questionable" (42). **Likewise, says Davis, he too must decide "whether or not there is compelling reason to reject some Biblical claim. For me this does not occur often, but it does occur occasionally. It has never yet occurred on a matter of faith or practice, and, like Fuller, I hope it never will" (76).**

In the midst of all this subjectivity, relativity, and uncertainty, Davis makes his final appeal to the most subjective criterion of all: the inner guidance of the Holy Spirit. "I do affirm the traditional Christian claim that the Holy Spirit guides us into truth, although I do not wish to explore here the question of how this guidance works in relation to Scripture, reason, or any other epistemological authority" (72).

In the final analysis, when human experience replaces the Bible as our ultimate norm, whether it be collective or personal experience, the Bible is *demoted* and takes a secondary place. It is used when convenient to lend authority to the ideas and priorities absorbed and applied from the contemporary culture, or from one's own independent reasoning and judgment, in the name of the Holy Spirit.

How is this affecting "our" churches today? It means that *liberalism* is making definite inroads into our Movement, both in our churches and in our schools. This is happening in two ways. First, we have a growing number of church leaders who have openly rejected the inerrancy of Scripture and along with it the very concept of sound doctrine. All but a handful of beliefs are considered to be matters of opinion, leaving the door wide open to ecumenism. We can think of this as "theoretical liberalism."

But there is something else that is more common, something we may call "practical liberalism." Here I am referring to folks (and churches) who may not specifically deny the inerrancy of the Bible, folks who may formally adhere to the complete authority of the Bible, but who simply do not USE the Bible in any serious way in their lives and perhaps even in their churches. The Bible has been, for all practical purposes, demoted and neglected. The result is PRACTICAL liberalism.

This practical liberalism can take many forms. For example, church services as such, under the influence of the "seeker sensitive" model, have often been reduced to entertainment, aimed at feelings more than the intellect, in the attempt to produce a "feel-good" experience.

Also, sermons may be harvested from on-line sermon sites and preached without conviction. Little time is spent in real Bible study and exegesis. Serious doctrinal subjects are avoided. The result is what Edith Schaeffer once compared with flavored "sawdust sandwiches": very tasty but lacking nutritional value. (People sometimes ask me: what books or authors do you read or recommend? My main answer is that the bookshelves surrounding my work desk at home are filled with Bible versions, Greek and Hebrew study helps, reference works [including *The Faith Once for All*, of course!], and some commentaries.)

What about "Sunday" School? Attendance is usually atrocious. Study materials are often not the Bible itself or even serious Bible study works, but light, fluffy stuff by denominational authors. And often, not only do the church leaders not attend, but they do not encourage others to do so.

Our church resources in general—periodicals, conferences, teachers, preachers—often tend to focus on "how-to" materials and subjects, such as leadership skills, family issues, church activities, and church growth. Many avoid taking a stand on any controversial Bible doctrine—especially baptism, for fear of offending someone and driving away potential and even current members. Keep everyone happy, and watch those attendance numbers climb!

When we no longer make the Word of God a major center of our lives and our church life, we are not just letting dust gather on the Bible as a book lying on a shelf somewhere. We are actually insulting the *author* of that book: the Holy Spirit. We are *grieving* "the Holy Spirit of God" (Ephesians 4:30). We are slighting the most wonderful gift that the Spirit has given to mankind! We are joining the ranks of the liberals through our practical liberalism.

IV. RESTORING THE HOLY SPIRIT'S MAIN WORK IN THE CHURCH

Many decry the absence of the Holy Spirit in their lives and in their churches. (See, for example, Francis Chan's book, *Forgotten God.*) So do I. I deplore two common errors in our churches regarding the work of the Holy Spirit. (1) One, it is possible to be guilty of LIMITING the work of the Holy Spirit to what He does through the Bible. We do this when we fail to see the marvelous ways He is working in us for salvation purposes. (2) Two, it is possible to be guilty of SEPARATING the work of the Holy Spirit from the role and use of the Bible (often as an overreaction to the former). The latter is the problem I am focusing on here.

Do you want the Holy Spirit to play a bigger role in your life and in the life of your church? Here's where to start: USE THE BIBLE MORE, AND USE IT RIGHT! The Holy Spirit works in very important ways in *addition* to how He works through the Bible, but it all *starts* with how He works therein. Let's start restoring the Spirit's main work in the church by recovering and teaching with firm conviction that the Bible IS the Spirit-inspired Word of God, true and without error in all it affirms, the only rule of faith and practice. (Do Christians today know where this is taught in the Bible itself?)

Also, let's see how we can build our lives and churches more openly around the authority and contents of the Bible. I challenge us as church leaders to set the example. I urge you to provide Bible study options that set forth the meat of the Word, and I urge you to be proactive in insisting that the members of your flock participate in these study opportunities and responsibilities.

PART TWO:
THE BIBLE VS. PENTECOSTALISM

INTRODUCTION

In the previous essay I distinguished the four kinds of gifts God's people receive from the Holy Spirit: *truth* gifts, *sign* gifts, *service* gifts, and *salvation* gifts. A major key to understanding the work of the Holy Spirit, and of sorting out these kinds of gifts, is *a right understanding of the Day of Pentecost* as recorded in the second chapter of Acts. Presenting this understanding of Pentecost is the goal of this present essay.

I.   THE PROMISE OF A NEW WORK OF THE SPIRIT

The first thing that is necessary for a proper understanding of Pentecost is to be aware of the long string of God's promises and prophecies of a *new work* of the Holy Spirit that would come in God's chosen time. The main point of these promises is that on that coming day, the Spirit is going to do *something new!* And we now understand that this new work of the Spirit is something that began on the Day of Pentecost as described in Acts 2. Here are the texts that embody these promises:

- **Isaiah 43:19-21; 44:3-4** – Behold, I will do something new, now it will spring forth; Will you not be aware of it? I will even make a roadway in the wilderness, rivers in the desert. The beasts of the field will glorify Me, the jackals and the ostriches, because I have given waters in the wilderness and rivers in the desert, to give drink to My chosen people. The people whom I formed for Myself will declare My praise.… For I will pour out water on the thirsty land and streams on the dry ground; I will pour out My Spirit on your offspring and My blessing on your descendants; and they will spring up among the grass like poplars by streams of water.

- **Ezekiel 36:25-27** – Then I will sprinkle clean water on you, and you will be clean; I will cleanse you from all your filthiness and from all your idols. Moreover, I will give you a new heart and put a new spirit within you; and I will remove the heart of stone from your flesh and give you a heart of flesh. I will put My Spirit within you and cause you to walk in My statutes, and you will be careful to observe my ordinances.

- **Joel 2:28-32** – It will come about after this that I will pour out My Spirit on all mankind; and your sons and daughters will prophesy, your old men will dream dreams, your young men will see visions. Even on the male and female servants I will pour out my Spirit in those days. I will display wonders in the sky and on the earth, blood, fire and columns of smoke. The sun will be turned into darkness and the moon into blood before the great and awesome day of the LORD comes. And it will come about that whoever calls on the name of the LORD will be delivered. For on Mount Zion and in Jerusalem there will be those who escape, as the LORD has said, even among the survivors whom the LORD calls.

- **Matthew 3:11** (John the Baptist says) – "As for me, I baptize you with water for repentance, but He who is coming after me is mightier than I, and I am not fit to remove His sandals; He will baptize you with the Holy Spirit and fire." (See Luke 3:16.)

- **John 1:33** – (Also from John the Baptist) "I did not recognize Him, but He who sent me to baptize in water said to me, 'He upon whom you see the Spirit descending and remaining upon Him, this is the One who baptizes in the Holy Spirit.'"

- **John 4:7-14** – There came a woman of Samaria to draw water. Jesus said to her, "Give Me a drink." For His disciples had gone away into the city to buy food. Therefore the Samaritan woman said to Him, "How is it that You, being a Jew, ask me for a drink since I am a Samaritan woman?" (For Jews have no dealings with Samaritans.) Jesus answered and said to her, "If you knew the gift of God, and who it is who says to you, 'Give Me a drink,' you would have asked Him, and He would have given you living water." She said to Him, "Sir, You have nothing to draw with and the well is deep; where then do You get that living water? You are not greater than our father Jacob, are You, who gave us the well, and drank of it himself and his sons and cattle?" Jesus answered and said to her, "Everyone who drinks of this water will thirst again; but whoever drinks of the water that I will give him shall never thirst; but the water that I will give him will become in him a well of water springing up to eternal life."

- **John 7:37-39** – Now on the last day, the great day of the feast, Jesus stood and cried out, saying, "If anyone is thirsty, let him come to Me and drink. He who believes in Me, as the Scripture said, 'From his innermost being will flow rivers of living water.'" But this He spoke of the Spirit, whom those who believed in Him were to receive; for the Spirit was not yet given, because Jesus was not yet glorified.

- **Acts 1:4-8** – Gathering them together, He commanded them not to leave Jerusalem, but to wait for what the Father had promised, "Which," He said, "you heard of from Me; for John baptized with water, but you will be baptized with the Holy Spirit not many days from now." So when they had come together, they were asking Him, saying, "Lord, is it at this time You are restoring the kingdom to Israel?" He said to them, "It is not for you to know times or epochs which the Father has fixed by His own authority; but you will receive power when the Holy Spirit has come upon you; and you shall be My witnesses both in Jerusalem, and in all Judea and Samaria, and even to the remotest part of the earth."

All of these texts are all pointing ahead to the same thing, the same NEW thing. They point to a blessing truly grand and wonderful, something of tremendous magnitude, something that will be characteristic of the whole New Covenant age. Indeed, they point to a *distinguishing element* of the church age: a *new kind* of gift of the Holy Spirit. This is the *one thing* that makes the Messianic era unique. This age in which we live, the post-Pentecostal age, is *the era of the Holy Spirit.*

The language of Joel's prophecy, in vv. 30-31 (quoted in Acts 2:19-20), gives us a clue as to the time when this new thing would begin. This is a kind of apocalyptic language: "wonders in the sky and on the earth, blood, fire and columns of smoke"; the sun "turned into darkness and the moon into blood." Such language was sometimes used in prophecy to indicate decisive transitions in history, especially the downfall of a nation. (See, e.g., Isaiah 13:10; 34:4-5; Ezekiel 32:7-8; Matthew 24:29-31.) The nation whose "downfall" is being symbolized by this language is *Israel itself,* whose place as the chosen nation came to an end with the beginning of the New Covenant, which was officially launched on the Day of Pentecost. From that point on, the Church of Jesus Christ has been God's chosen people.

How does this relate to the four kinds of gifts given by the Holy Spirit (truth, sign, service, salvation)? What does this *new* thing, highlighted in these prophecies and promises, have to do with these gifts? And how do they relate to Pentecost?

The fact is that only *three* of these kinds of gifts existed before Pentecost. The *truth* gifts of revelation and inspiration were certainly in effect, as God's Spirit spoke through those chosen to relay God's inspired Word to His people. See, for example, 2 Samuel 23:2, and the many other texts quoted in the previous essay. Also, *sign* gifts, i.e., miracles, were given to individuals such as Moses, Elijah, and the apostles themselves (Matthew 10:1, 8; Luke 9:1). See especially Numbers 11:16ff. It is very important to see that miracles were already present before Pentecost. Finally, *service* gifts were also given before Pentecost. See Exodus 31:1-11; Numbers 11:16ff.

However, the one kind of gift that was *not* being given by the Spirit prior to Pentecost was the *salvation* gifts. When we understand this, it becomes possible to sort out what the Holy Spirit was actually doing on the Day of Pentecost.

II. THE PENTECOSTAL WORKS OF THE SPIRIT

Our question now is this: exactly what was the Holy Spirit doing on the Day of Pentecost, as recorded in Acts 2? The fact is that he was doing several kinds of things, but the crucial point is to see which of these was the NEW thing.

The one kind of gift that is not specifically mentioned as being manifested on Pentecost is *service* gifts, in the sense of ordinary spiritual gifts such as are listed in Romans 12:7-8. But even if some were present on that day, they would not be something new.

We can definitely identify the presence of the *truth* gift, though. Just as Jesus promised in John 14-16 that the Holy Spirit would come upon

His apostles to give them "all the truth" (John 16:13), so does the Apostle Peter speak an inspired message of truth when he preaches his Pentecostal sermon in Acts 2:14-40. This inspired "apostles' teaching" continued from that time on (Acts 2:42). But even though new content was given through the apostles' inspired teaching, this cannot be the fulfillment of the prophecies and promises about a NEW thing, a NEW work of the Spirit. This *kind* of inspired teaching had been done often before, throughout the Old Testament era, as evidenced by the very existence of the Old Testament Scriptures.

What about *sign* gifts on the Day of Pentecost? Herein lies the source of much confusion. Yes, there was a major sign gift given on the Day of Pentecost, i.e., the *speaking in tongues* recorded in Acts 2:1-13. This was a true miracle, in the form of the ability to speak clearly in languages that were unlearned and unknown by those who spoke them.

The key question about the speaking in tongues is this: what was the *purpose* for which the Holy Spirit gave this ability to (probably) just the Apostles on the Day of Pentecost? The purpose was NOT to enable them to communicate the gospel to those in the audience who spoke a myriad of languages (see Acts 2:8-11). This is a common assumption, but it is a serious misunderstanding. The *content* of the message given through tongues was not the point. There is no indication whatsoever that the subject of this speaking had anything at all to do with Jesus and the gospel. Rather, the apostles spoke of known things, "the mighty works of God" (v. 11). This no doubt refers to the works of God recorded in the Old Testament Scriptures, events with which the Jews who were present would be quite familiar.

We should also remember that even though those in the audience were Jews who spoke a multiplicity of languages, they also spoke the common language of Greek. Thus there was no need to use their native tongues if the content was the point. All could talk among themselves (see vv. 7-13); they all understood Peter's sermon (v. 37).

No, the gift of tongues was not a *truth* gift on this occasion, but a *sign* gift. The purpose was to present an obvious *miracle*, which functioned as a SIGN (evidence, proof) of the TRUTH of the message Peter was about to preach to them. The miracle had the intended effect: the audience was bewildered, amazed, astonished, perplexed (vv. 6, 7, 12). (Two parallel events can be mentioned: (1) the miraculous prophesying done by Moses's assistants in Numbers 11:16ff.; and (2) the speaking in tongues by Cornelius and his family in Acts 10:44ff. In both these cases the point of the miraculous speaking was to give divine proof of an accompanying message or promise.)

Here is the common but critical error of Pentecostals, Charismatics, and still many Restorationists, namely, they assume that the tongue-speaking in Acts 2 was the *big deal*, the main point, the highlight of Pentecost. The Pentecostals and Charismatics assume it was the beginning of a new and permanent blessing intended for the church until the end of time; the Restorationists say it happened only one other time (with Cornelius), but it was still the big deal about Pentecost anyway. BOTH ARE WRONG. We must *stop* thinking of the tongues as the climactic event of Pentecost.

Remember: this *kind* of thing – a sign gift, an exhibition of miraculous power – was *nothing new*! *WHY SHOULD THE MIRACULOUS MANIFESTATIONS ON PENTECOST BE CONSIDERED THE ESSENCE OF THE NEW-AGE OUTPOURING OF THE HOLY SPIRIT? THIS KIND OF THING WAS <u>NOTHING NEW</u>!*

So what IS the new work of the Holy Spirit, beginning on Pentecost? It is the *salvation* gifts, associated with the "gift of the Holy Spirit" promised by Peter in Acts 2:38. The tongue-speaking raised the question, "What's going on here?" Peter's sermon answers that question.

III. HOW DOES PETER EXPLAIN THE TONGUES EVENT?

When Peter begins to preach his Pentecost sermon (Acts 2:14ff.), he begins by explaining that the tongue-speaking that got their attention was the fulfillment of prophecy, the prophecy given in Joel 2:28-32 concerning the promised coming of the Holy Spirit. He uses this prophecy to lead into the gospel facts about Jesus, namely, His death, resurrection, ascension, and lordship (Acts 2:22-36), then he uses these gospel facts about Jesus—especially his ascension and exaltation to the Father's right hand—to explain a new kind of presence of the Holy Spirit among God's people (Acts 2:33)! He says of Jesus, "Being therefore exalted at the right hand of God, and having received from the Father the promise of the Holy Spirit, he has poured out this that you yourselves are seeing and hearing" (2:33).

But this still leaves open the question, "So what?" The answer to that question comes when the audience asks Peter in verse 37, "Okay, so what are we supposed to do about this?" Peter's answer to this question (vv. 38-39) emphasizes not only their need for a relationship with Jesus Christ, but also their need for a relationship with the Holy Spirit: "And Peter said to them, 'Repent and be baptized every one of you in the name of Jesus Christ for the forgiveness of your sins, and you will receive the gift of the Holy Spirit. For the promise is for you and for your children and for all who are far off, everyone whom the Lord our God calls to himself.'"

The reference to baptism for the forgiveness of sins makes it easy for many of us to overlook the main point of this answer (vv. 38-39). But the fact is that what Peter says about the Holy Spirit is the main point! Remember: this whole discourse started with a query about the tongue-speaking, and Peter explains it by connecting it with the prophesied outpouring of the Holy Spirit. And he called attention to the fact that this outpouring of the Spirit was exactly what the Father had promised (v. 33). "And now you want to know what you should do about this? I'll tell you what: repent and be baptized in the name of Jesus for the forgiveness of your sins, *and you will receive this same Holy Spirit as the Father's personal gift to you!* That's what this is all about! The promised Spirit is among you this very moment! The tongue-speaking proves it! God is finally keeping His promise; and my friends, YOU just happen to be here when He is doing this! And He is doing it FOR YOU! FOR YOU is this promise of the Holy Spirit—and for the future generations after you—and even for the Gentiles! Wow!"

We need to pay more attention to verse 39. In the Greek the first words, in the emphatic position, are "FOR YOU!" "*For you* is the promise!" What promise? The promise of verse 33—the HOLY SPIRIT, whom Jesus received from the Father and has poured out all around you this very day!

Again, here is the essence of Peter's message in vv. 38-39 (imagine Peter speaking these words):

This is the day God has been promising for centuries; this is the day the Holy Spirit has been poured out like a virtual Niagara Falls. He is here among us, in a way He has never been present before! The miraculous events you have witnessed (wind, tongues of fire, speaking in tongues) are evidence of it. And the amazing thing is this: this NEW presence and gift of the Holy Spirit is FOR YOU – and for all your descendants, and even for the Gentiles!

And do you know the nature of this new gift of the Spirit? It is a SALVATION gift – the gift of the Holy Spirit HIMSELF, personally, to live within you and to empower you to live a holy life before the Father. This is a whole new way for the Holy Spirit to work among you, His people!

If you believe what I am telling you – and you should, because of the miraculous tongue-speaking, then you must repent of your sins and be baptized in the name of Jesus Christ for the forgiveness of your sins. If you do that, this gift – the Holy Spirit Himself – will be yours.

You will experience your *own personal Pentecost* when you obey the gospel in baptism!

On that last point, see Titus 3:3-7.

So—THIS is the big deal of Pentecost – not the tongues as such, not ANY sign gifts or miracles that may have occurred that day. (How many received the gift of the Holy Spirit that day? Three thousand! How many continued to do miracles after that? Twelve! See Acts 2:43; 3:6; 4:33; 5:12ff. There is no record of any Christians performing miracles until *after* the apostles began laying their hands on specific individuals, including Stephen and Philip—see Acts 6:1ff.)

CONCLUSION

There are many solid arguments against the continuation of *truth* gifts and *sign* gifts from the Holy Spirit after the Apostolic age, i.e., arguments that these sorts of gifts have ceased. See my books on the Holy Spirit. (*Power from on High: What the Bible Says About the Holy Spirit*, chs. 5, 11; *The Holy Spirit: A Biblical Study*, chs. 3, 8-10.)

I am not saying that God is not working in the world today. He is definitely intervening in the world in many powerful, supernatural ways. But I am saying that God's mighty works do not have to be *miraculous* events. The best understanding of Scripture is that God has not been giving miracle-working power to *individuals* after the apostolic age.

I believe that miracles are occurring in the world today, and that certain individuals do have miracle-working power, often even within Christian contexts. But I believe these powers are demonic in origin, and are the result of demonic deception. See 2 Thessalonians 2:9; Matthew 7:21-23.

I ask you to consider: what do we have to offer to the sinful world today? The same thing that Peter offered his audience on the Day of Pentecost. Did he offer them the power to work miracles? The chance to experience exciting miraculous powers flowing through them? NO! See again Matthew 7:21-23 on that! Let us be careful not to elevate experience above the Word of God! (See John MacArthur's books, *Charismatic Chaos* and *Strange Fire*.)

So what did Peter offer his audience on the day of Pentecost? Here is what he offered them: (pardon the expression—) HOPE and CHANGE! He offered them forgiveness of sins and thus an assured hope for eternal life in the *future*, and he offered them spiritual power to bring about change in their lives *now* through the brand new reality of the indwelling of the Holy Spirit! This latter point is the REAL Pentecostal power: *moral* power, not miraculous power.

We should not confuse the gift with the wrappings in which it arrived. Those today who still focus on the tongues aspect of Pentecost are like someone who receives a beautifully-wrapped birthday gift. After carefully removing the velvet ribbon and the expensive paper, the lovely box is opened to reveal the keys to a fancy new Mercedes automobile! But then this confused celebrant nonchalantly tosses aside these keys with a casual "That's nice." Then he turns back to the wrapping in which they came: "Wow! What wonderful ribbon!" he cries. "What beautiful paper! What a gorgeous box! I love it! I'm going to keep this ribbon and box and paper forever!"

The tongues were only the wrappings, to be laid aside so we can enjoy the permanent blessing of Pentecost: the salvation gift of the personal indwelling of the Holy Spirit.

PART THREE:
THE BIBLE VS. CALVINISM

INTRODUCTION

The issue here is how the Holy Spirit works upon the hearts of the unsaved, in order to bring them into a saved state. This is an unfolding of the first part of the SALVATION work of the Spirit that began on the Day of Pentecost.

I. TWO EXTREMES MUST BE AVOIDED

When we are thinking about how the Holy Spirit works prior to conversion, we must be careful to avoid two extremes. One extreme is Calvinism. The theological system of Calvinism says that the Holy Spirit, working *directly* upon the sinner's heart, is the only cause at work in bringing the sinner from a lost state to a saved state. (This is technically called "monergism," i.e., a term that means that there is only *one* agent *working* in conversion: the Holy Spirit.)

This view of salvation has two roots. One is the theological root, which is the doctrine of *total depravity*. This view began with Augustine (early fifth century), continued sporadically through the Middle Ages, and was adopted by the mainstream Protestant Reformers, including Martin Luther and John Calvin. This doctrine says that all human beings are conceived with a depraved (sinful) nature as the result of Adam's sin. The depravity is total in the sense that it affects all aspects of human nature, including the will. The result is *bondage* of the will, i.e., the total inability to respond to the gospel in faith and repentance. Total depravity is the "T" in Calvinism's T-U-L-I-P doctrines.

The other root of Calvinism's monergistic system is philosophical; it has to do with their understanding of the *sovereignty of God*. How Calvinists define divine sovereignty determines everything else about their system. God's sovereignty has to do with His kingship or lordship over all things. As Calvinists define it, divine sovereignty must be omnicausal (or pancausal), words that mean God is the ultimate *cause* of absolutely *everything*. This is how sovereignty is defined: God is sovereign *because* He initiates and is the true cause of everything. Otherwise He is not sovereign.

Either of these two starting points would in itself lead to monergism; both together make it absolutely inescapable. This leads to the "U" and the "I" in the T-U-L-I-P system, "unconditional election" and "irresistible grace." (This also guarantees the "P", or "perseverance of the saints," also called "once saved, always saved"; but here we are interested only in what happens in the sinner's experience *prior to* the moment when he or she becomes saved.) Unconditional election means that God is the only one who decides who will be saved and who will remain lost for eternity; no sinner has any choice in the matter. God determines from eternity past to save these chosen ones for eternity future. He determines to bring about their initial change of heart, and to make sure they never change back. Thus God exercises total causative control over the chosen ones' total existence and their total process of salvation.

Irresistible grace means that God alone determines and enacts every step of the actual process that brings the sinner into the saved state. At every point God is the only one who is working. This process must have a beginning, and here is where the Holy Spirit takes charge. At a single moment unilaterally selected by God, the Holy Spirit works *unilaterally*, *monergistically*, *irresistibly*, and *directly* upon the totally-depraved heart of the chosen one, and changes it from an unsaved state to a saved state.

The Calvinist says that four specific changes are included in this one divine act, this moment in which the Spirit touches the sinner's heart, in this logical order: (1) Regeneration, which is a change in the state of the heart itself. (2) Faith, i.e., the actual *creation* of faith in the heart. (3) Repentance: the actual creation of repentance in the heart. And (4) justification (forgiveness): a change of the status of the person before God. Each one of these is the direct work of the Holy Spirit.

The key change for our purposes is the first one, i.e., regeneration. In Calvinism this occurs solely by the power and operation of the Holy Spirit, without any conditions being met by the sinner, and without any preparation of the heart by the sinner himself or herself. In this event the Spirit works *directly* on the heart, "naked Spirit on naked spirit." Faith and repentance do not precede regeneration, but are the result of it. "Regeneration precedes faith" is the key element of the Calvinist idea of salvation.

Every aspect of salvation is thus a gift of the Holy Spirit. The Word of God is always a part of the salvation event, but how the sinner interacts with the Word is always under the Spirit's causative control.

The second extreme regarding how the Spirit works prior to conversion is one that is frequently found in the Restoration Movement, usually as an *overreaction* to Calvinism. This extreme view says that the ONLY way the Holy Spirit works on the sinner's heart is *indirectly*, through the power and influence of the Word of God. There is no direct working of the Spirit upon the sinner's heart.

Those who hold this view believe that salvation does require a change in the sinner's heart called "regeneration," or "being born again" (the new birth), or spiritual death to sin followed by resurrection to a new spiritual life. This change is indeed attributed to the Holy Spirit, *but* – in effecting this change the Holy Spirit is said to work ONLY indirectly, ONLY through the power and influence of the Word of God as it moves the sinner's heart and motivates the sinner to change himself. Since the Holy Spirit is the one who gave us the Bible, whatever is accomplished by the Bible is actually accomplished by the Holy Spirit Himself – but only *indirectly*.

Thus, in bringing about the conversion of the sinner, the Holy Spirit operates indirectly only, and never directly upon the heart. In fact, any kind of *direct* operation is seen as impossible, and it is also seen as a concession to Calvinism.

This was one of Alexander Campbell's main points in his 1844 debate with the Calvinist, N. L. Rice. In this debate Campbell says it is "an incontrovertible fact, that no light is communicated by the Holy Spirit, in regenerating and converting men, which is equivalent to saying that 'in conversion and sanctification the Spirit of God operates only through the Word of Truth'" (p. 620). See my book, *Power from on High*, 215-220, for the details of Campbell's view.

What, then, is the nature or essence of this "regeneration," this change wrought upon the sinner's heart by the Word of God (according to the Campbellian view)? Usually it is equated with the sinner's own action, the sinner's own decision to believe and repent. Regeneration IS the change the sinner undergoes when he believes and repents, as motivated by the gospel, the Word of God. It is not seen as some distinct and direct act of the Spirit *after* and *upon the condition of* the sinner's choice to believe and repent. That would somehow be the same as Calvinism! See *Power from on High*, 219-220.

In the final analysis, since regeneration is actually equated with the sinner's own actions of believing and repenting, for all practical purposes *the sinner regenerates himself!*

Here are some further examples of this view (besides A. Campbell and other 19th century Restoration Movement writers).

- Garth Black, *The Holy Spirit*, rev. ed., "The Way of Life" series (Abilene: Biblical Research Press, 1973), 27-28: He asserts "that the Holy Spirit operates in conversion only through the instrumentality of the word," as taught in such texts as Romans 1:16; 10:17. He concludes, "From these scriptures it is evident that the Holy Spirit operates upon the heart of the sinner in conversion through the truth, and that truth is the gospel message, the word of God. The New Testament does not teach that the Holy Spirit operates in any other way in conversion than through the instrumentality of the word."

- This includes those who see the death to sin and resurrection to new life in Romans 6:3-5 as equivalent to the sinner's acts of faith and repentance, which occur before baptism. Examples include Moses Lard, Don DeWelt, K. C. Moser, and David Lipscomb. (See my references to their views in my commentary on Romans.)

- A few years ago I received an email from a Restoration brother named Ray Downen (Joplin, MO) entitled "Does it matter who saves sinners?" In it Downen strongly attacks my view (taken from my book on baptism) that the new birth in John 3:5 is a work of the Holy Spirit. He says, "The new birth is of water and spirit rather than being of water and the Holy Spirit. It's accomplished by sinners hearing the Word of Christ (the gospel about Jesus) and surrendering to His Lordship." "What is involved in the new birth of water and spirit?" "It's repentance and baptism." "I repeat—the Spirit is NOT the cause of new birth."

- After I had been teaching for a few years at Cincinnati Bible Seminary that the Holy Spirit works directly upon the sinner's heart in regeneration, several faculty members (followers of A. Campbell on this point) tried in vain to get me fired. I was actually called before the president and the chairman of the board of trustees to answer for this Calvinist "heresy."

II. THE SPIRIT WORKS UPON THE HEARTS OF SINNERS BOTH INDIRECTLY AND DIRECTLY

Here I will show that the Holy Spirit, prior to the moment the sinner becomes saved, works upon his or her heart both indirectly and directly.

A. The INDIRECT Work of the Spirit on the Sinner's Heart

First, the Spirit works *indirectly* through the Word of God to bring about faith and repentance (which will then lead to confession and baptism). Campbell and others are right, that faith and repentance are produced by the Holy Spirit only indirectly, by means of the Word of God. Contrary to Calvinism, faith is NOT a unilateral, unconditional gift of the Holy Spirit. The Word motivates us, moves us, convicts us to believe (and repent) through the power of its message. This is indirectly the Spirit's work, since He is the ultimate origin of the Word; but here it is the Word that works directly upon the heart.

We can see how this should be the case once we understand the nature of faith. Faith is a two-fold change of the mind and heart about Jesus. It is first of all an act of the mind, an act of *assent*, or "believing THAT" something is true (e.g., John 20:30-31; Romans 10:9). Assent is a judgment of the intellect that certain statements are true. In the second place, faith is an act of the will, and act of *trust*, or "believing IN or ON" a person (e.g., John 3:16; Acts 16:31). Trust is a decision of the will to submit/commit to the person of Jesus.

Repentance is likewise a change of the mind and heart – about SIN. The Greek word *metanoia* (repentance) literally means "a change of the mind." It involves (1) a change of heart from loving sin, to a hatred of and disgust toward sin; and (2) a change of will from wanting to sin to a desire and determination NOT to sin.

What has the power to generate such changes within us? The Word of God. Hebrews 4:12 says that "the word of God is living and active and sharper than any two-edged sword, and piercing as far as the division of soul and spirit, of both joints and marrow, and able to judge the thoughts and intentions of the heart." Romans 1:16 says that the gospel "is the power of God for salvation to everyone who believes," and Romans 10:17 says that "faith *comes* from hearing, and hearing by the word of Christ." See also John 20:30-31 and John 12:32. An example of this power of the Word is Peter's Pentecost sermon. Acts 2:37 says that when he got to a certain point, his audience was "pierced to the heart" and requested information on what to do to be saved. This is the power of the Word.

At the same time, because of free will—contra Calvinism—the power of the Word thus can be resisted. See also Matthew 23:37, where Jesus says, "Jerusalem, Jerusalem, who kills the prophets and stones those who are sent to her! How often I wanted to gather your children together, the way a hen gathers her chicks under her wings, and you were unwilling." See Acts 7, which shows that Stephen's audience reacted to his sermon in a very different way from the way Peter's audience reacted to his sermon in Acts 2. Stephen describes them as "stiff-necked people, uncircumcised in heart and ears," and ones who "always resist the Holy Spirit" (7:51).

We see, then, that the Spirit does work, though indirectly, through the Word in order to bring the sinner to faith and repentance. However, faith and repentance themselves are NOT the essence of regeneration. This requires a *direct* work of the Spirit, as the following shows.

B.   The DIRECT Work of the Spirit on the Sinner's Heart

Once the Holy Spirit has worked through the Word of God to move the sinner to believe and to repent, the Word will then instruct the repentant sinner to obey the gospel by confessing Christ as Savior and Lord (Romans 10:9-10) and by being baptized for the forgiveness of sins (Acts 2:38). It is in the event of Christian baptism that the Holy Spirit works *directly* on the sinner's heart. This is the very purpose of the gift of the indwelling Spirit promised in baptism. This direct working of the Spirit is the beginning of the NEW WORK that had been promised ever since Isaiah, Ezekiel, and Joel, and then promised by John the Baptist and Jesus! THIS IS THE INITIAL STEP OF THE NEW WORK OF THE HOLY SPIRIT THAT BEGAN ON PENTECOST.

What is this new, direct work of the Holy Spirit? Most often in theological discussion it is called regeneration, which is what Paul calls it in Titus 3:5: God "saved us, not on the basis of deeds which we have done in righteousness, but according to His mercy, by **the washing of regeneration** and renewing by the Holy Spirit." It is also called being born again (John 3:5); being spiritually circumcised (Colossians 2:11); being created anew (2 Corinthians 5:17); and undergoing death to sin and resurrection to new spiritual life (Romans 6:3-5; Colossians 2:12-13).

When we say that this is a direct work of the Spirit upon the sinner's heart, we are saying that it is a "naked Spirit on naked spirit" work, in which the Holy Spirit touches our spirit for the purpose of bringing it back to spiritual life again, or for the purpose of beginning the process of healing that will continue throughout the Christian life (a process called sanctification).

The truth is this: the Calvinist error is NOT that this work of regeneration is a *direct* work of the Holy Spirit; rather, the error is *when* and *for what purpose* the Spirit does such work. Assuming total depravity, the Calvinist believes that the sinner can do nothing to prepare for and consent to this coming of the Spirit; the Calvinist believes that this direct act of regeneration is not just an act of salvation itself, but that it bestows the very presence of faith and repentance that logically must precede regeneration. This is the error that must be rejected.

But we must also reject the common Restoration Movement error that this Biblical regeneration is something that the sinner can and must do for himself or herself. The sinner cannot will himself to be born again:

we are spiritually reborn "not of blood nor of the will of the flesh nor of the will of man, but of God" (John 1:13). We are born again "of water and the Spirit" (John 3:5). This new birth, or regeneration, is *the saving work of God the Holy Spirit*. We were "buried with him in baptism, in which [we] were also raised with him **through faith in the powerful working of God**" (Colossians 2:12, ESV).

This is not something we mortals can do; only God the Holy Spirit can do it! It is actually described in Ezekiel 36:25-27 as a heart transplant! I am reminded of this every time I think of the King James Version of Colossians 2:12, which says that in baptism we are raised up with Christ through "faith in the OPERATION of God." Yes indeed—a heart transplant! Friends, when you undergo a serious operation, you can and must submit yourself to the surgeon, as the result of your own free-will choice. But the real work is done by the surgeon, who himself does two things. First, he explains (gives you the knowledge of) your need for the surgery, and of what is going to take place when you are on the operating table. (This is comparable to the role of the Word in preparing us for Holy Spirit regeneration.) Then the surgeon performs the actual operation (which is comparable to the direct work of the Holy Spirit on the sinner's heart in baptism).

The Bible is very clear that the Holy Spirit's saving work of regeneration is done in baptism. This is one reason we think of baptism as a salvation event, as a work of God. See John 3:5; Titus 3:5; Acts 2:38; 1 Corinthians 12:13.

Here is a point we need to get used to: this regenerating work of the Holy Spirit is what the Bible calls "being baptized in the Holy Spirit." "Baptism in the Holy Spirit" is not for the purpose of giving miraculous powers, but for the purpose of salvation. And this baptism in the Spirit is not a saving act that is separate from water baptism. Rather, baptism in water and baptism in the Spirit occur simultaneously, as two parts of the ONE BAPTISM of Ephesians 4:5. Baptism has an outside (water) and an inside (the Spirit). See John 3:5 and Hebrews 10:22. We need to take 1 Corinthians 12:13 seriously: "For by one Spirit we were all baptized into one body, whether Jews or Greeks, whether slaves or free, and we were all made to drink of one Spirit."

We must abandon the idea that baptism in the Holy Spirit (Acts 1:5) is referring to the sign-event of Acts 2:1-13, i.e., the gift of tongues given for evidential purposes. That was not a new kind of thing. The baptism in the Spirit was a new thing, a salvation gift applied in baptism (Acts 2:38-39), one that is still continuing today.

What is the result of this work of regeneration? We now have MORAL POWER, power over sin, power to live a holy life (sanctification), power over our sin-indwelt bodies (Romans 6:6-14), power to put sin to death in our lives (Romans 8:13). This is not a complete, 100% healing accomplished in a single moment, but the beginning of a life-long process. It is the reversal of the general direction of one's life. It is the beginning of a process of further change, which is the lifelong healing process known as sanctification.

Regeneration is similar to an event often depicted in old Western movies where a principal in the story would be wounded and develop an infection and a fever. With no antibiotics the local doctor could only monitor the sick man's condition until either the latter died or "the fever broke," as they would say. The time when "the fever broke" was the turning point, the beginning of the wounded man's recovery. Likewise, regeneration is the time when the sin-fever breaks and the life-giving power of the Holy Spirit sets the sinner on the road to spiritual wholeness.

Or to use the medical analogy again, now that you have been regenerated, the medicine (i.e., the Holy Spirit) is IN you, and has begun and is continuing to work on you. You have drunk the "living water" (1 Corinthians 12:13b) and He has brought your dead soul back to life; He has broken the curse of spiritual death upon your soul. (See John 7:35-37; Ephesians 2:1-5; Colossians 2:12-13.)

PART FOUR:
THE BIBLE VS. MYSTICISM

INTRODUCTION

In this essay I am using the term "mysticism" in a very general, non-technical sense. I am using it to refer to the common idea that truth is to be found not in the outside, objective world, but coming from within ourselves. This is the opposite of the theme of the old televison show, "The X-files" – "The truth is OUT THERE." The theme of mysticism is – "The truth is IN HERE," inside ourselves.

According to mysticism, truth (or knowledge) is *subjective*. If you want to know the truth, you have to look within yourself. It is like the well-known poster seen on a college campus, advertising a sect of Eastern mysticism: "You go in and in and in. And then you go in and in and in. And after that you go in and in and in."

Here I am specifically addressing one of the most common errors Christians make about the Holy Spirit. It has to do with the main purpose for the indwelling of the Spirit within us.

I said in the first session that the Holy Spirit gives us two main kinds of gifts: gifts of knowledge and gifts of power. How does this apply to the reason God has given us the gift of the *indwelling presence* of the Spirit in baptism? What is the Holy Spirit doing for us NOW?

A common idea is that somehow, the Spirit dwells within us to give us KNOWLEDGE. I am not even talking about Pentecostal or Charismatic gifts of knowledge, such as the gift of prophecy. I am talking about the ordinary concept of the indwelling of the Spirit, and the fact that many Christians assume that

- when they need to know the will of God, or
- when they need to know what a specific passage of the Bible means, or
- when they need to know what to do in any given difficult situation

– all they have to do is LOOK WITHIN, to "go in and in and in," and find within themselves the very voice of God speaking to them through the indwelling of the Holy Spirit.

I want to be very emphatic about this: this is a VERY serious misunderstanding of the work of the Holy Spirit! The NEW gift of the Spirit, begun on Pentecost, is a wonderful gift indeed. To have the very Spirit of God dwelling in us is enough to fill us with reverential fear and trembling (Philippians 2:12)! But we need to get straight on WHY HE IS HERE! The bottom line is this: We do not have the Spirit within us to give us *knowledge*; He is within us to give us POWER – a very specific kind of power. That is the burden of this lesson.

I.   THE FACT OF THE SPIRIT'S INDWELLING

First, let us be clear that the Holy Spirit does dwell within us, literally and personally, from the moment of our baptism and following.

- **Ezekiel 36:27** – "I will put my Spirit within you."
- **John 7:38** – "He who believes in me, as the Scripture said, from his innermost being will flow rivers of living water."
- **1 Corinthians 6:19** – "Do you not know that your body is a temple of the Holy Spirit who is in you, whom you have from God?"

- **Romans 8:9-11** – "However, you are not in the flesh but in the Spirit, if indeed the Spirit of God dwells in you. But if anyone does not have the Spirit of Christ, he does not belong to Him. If Christ is in you, though the body is dead because of sin, yet the spirit is alive because of righteousness. But if the Spirit of Him who raised Jesus from the dead dwells in you, He who raised Christ Jesus from the dead will also give life to your mortal bodies through His Spirit who dwells in you."
- **Galatians 4:6** – "God has sent forth the Spirit of His Son into our hearts."
- **2 Timothy 1:14** – "The Holy Spirit … dwells in us."

Now the question is: WHY?

II.   THE WRONG ANSWER: FOR KNOWLEDGE

As indicated above: a common (but erroneous) assumption is that God gives us the indwelling of the Spirit in order to give us *knowledge*. This error takes several forms. For example, a very common mistake, sometimes even by scholars, is to take Biblical promises that were originally intended for the *apostles* (such as John 16:13), or statements that originally applied only to inspired apostles and prophets (such as 1 Corinthians 2:9-16), and assume that they were intended to apply to all Christians. I will give some examples of this false view.

One such example is the respected Evangelical scholar, Leon Morris, in his book, *Spirit of the Living God* (London: IVP, 1960). Commenting on John 16:13, he says that "the Christian has a wonderful promise from the Master Himself…. This gives a general charter which we may claim in all sorts of situations." Just as the apostles spoke by and were guided by the Spirit in the Book of Acts, so "the Spirit does guide us. He does show us the way in which we should go. He does give the words that are necessary when we need His help" (pp. 78-79).

An earlier scholar, R. A. Torrey, says much the same thing in his book, *The Person and Work of the Holy Spirit* (Revell, 1910). Citing John 14:26 and John 16:12-14, he declares that "in all these passages it is perfectly clear that the Holy Spirit is ... a Person who comes to us to teach us day by day the truth of God. It is the privilege of the humblest believer ... to have a Divine Teacher to daily teach him the truth he needs to know" (pp. 18-19). "We shall never truly know the truth until we are thus taught directly by the Holy Spirit" (p. 144).

In a letter to *Christian Standard* a writer said that "the same Holy Spirit that told holy men of old what to write in the Bible also indwells Christians today and continues to prompt, lead, and speak to us." Texts cited to confirm this claim included 1 Corinthians 2:12-13 and John 16:13. The writer said that such leading and speaking "does not mean we are receiving new revelation" (Chris Criminger, "Don't Lock [the] Holy Spirit in [the] Bible," May 1, 1994, p. 23).

I was teaching an adult Bible class in a Cincinnati area church some years ago when the subject of the need and use of the Bible was raised. A man in the class—a deacon and the church treasurer—literally declared that Christians no longer need the Bible because we have the Holy Spirit.

I cannot emphasize enough how mistaken this view is.

But that's not all. Another common error is to adopt the false doctrine called *illumination*, originally grounded in Calvinism and now found in most Protestantism. This is the belief that depravity (total or partial) has rendered all human beings incapable of understanding the true meaning of any Biblical text without divine help. Therefore, one of the Spirit's functions as a result of his indwelling is to "illuminate" our minds so that we are able to understand what the Bible means. Thus we must continue to seek this knowledge and to pray for the Spirit to provide it.

Here are some examples. First, some time ago I read about a Christian worker who tells of spending two months in confinement waiting for a broken leg to heal, and of using that time just reading the Bible, "with no commentary of man but rather looking to the Holy Spirit to open my eyes to spiritual understanding." Another example is the Bible college professor who writes that "the Holy Spirit's purpose here is to teach us Jesus and to reveal the meaning of Scripture."

Years ago I was on a task force attempting to come to an understanding of the Bible's teaching on gender roles. One member of the task force asked, "Why can't I just trust the Holy Spirit to lead me into the truth on this subject without my having to read what others have written on it?" Another Christian lady said she "felt led to write" me a letter, in which she said that 2 Peter 1:20-21 "notes the Holy Spirit as *author* and *interpreter* of Scriptures." A "workers ready for service" request in the old *Christian Standard* said, "Inexperienced minister looking for small church.... Has ... never been to college but is guided by the Holy Spirit." (Gr-o-o-o-a-n!!)

Another common but erroneous approach is to focus on passages that talk about how we are "led by the Holy Spirit" (e.g., Romans 8:14), and to interpret them to mean that the Holy Spirit gives us inner guidance on decision-making and knowing the best choices when we face difficult situations.

Many have learned this approach from the Evangelical writer Francis Chan, especially from his book, *Forgotten God: Reversing Our Tragic Neglect of the Holy Spirit* (David C. Cook, 2009). In this book he says that one thing the indwelling Spirit does for us is this: "The Counselor teaches and reminds us of what we need to know and remember .... He guides us in the way we should go." Here he cites John 14-16 and 1 Corinthians 2:9-10 as Biblical proof (pp. 74-75).

Chan goes on to say the following: "The Holy Spirit was given to direct us. Desiring the Holy Spirit means we allow the Holy Spirit to guide us" (89). Do you *really* want him to lead you? "What if He leads you where you don't want to go? What if he tells you to change jobs? To move?" Will you follow? Sometimes "He calls us to do something, a particular thing, and we have the choice to obey or not" (90). "God wants us to listen to His Spirit on a daily basis, ... as difficult ... moments arise, and in the midst of the mundane." I should "learn to seek hard after 'the Spirit's leading in my life today'" (120-21). "The Spirit may lead me into total sacrifice financially.... The Spirit may ask me to move to a different city, a different state, or a different country. The Spirit may ask me to stay where I can and spend my time in very different ways than I do now" (126-127).

Another example of this false view is Gary Zustiak, in an article in *Christian Standard* ("Hearing the Voice of God," Oct. 24, 1999, 4-6). He said that Hebrews 1:1-2 does not eliminate the possibility of continuing "individual guidance and direction" from God "in matters of personal decision-making." Over time, one can "learn to recognize God's voice." When He speaks, "not only will God's voice be clear, but it will be specific." Of course, "whatever God speaks to us, it will never contradict what has already been written in the Bible."

Bob Russell, in a *Lookout* article called "How God Speaks" (Sept. 1, 2002, p. 14), tells of a man who brought him occasional messages from God, e.g., "God spoke to me last night and told me I should share this Scripture with you." Russell expressed to the man his doubts about such claims to verbal revelation today. The man was undaunted. He said that God had spoken to him and revealed that his estranged wife would return to him within two weeks. The man disappeared but then reappeared six months later and declared, "God spoke to me several months ago and told me I needed to go to another church." Unfortunately, his wife had not returned to him, but he was still listening to these "messages from God."

Regarding all of these attempts to find knowledge from the indwelling Spirit by looking to some kind of inner voice or inward impressions, I say NO! This is NOT the point of the indwelling of the Holy Spirit! The most basic thing to understand about the work of the Holy Spirit is this: the only *knowledge* we get from the Holy Spirit comes from the BIBLE! (See the first lesson in this series.) Let us avoid mysticism, i.e., looking within ourselves for knowledge. Our knowledge is OBJECTIVE, not subjective.

Let's be very clear about this: Biblical promises meant for the apostles and prophets must NOT be applied to all Christians. This especially is true of Jesus's private discussion with His apostles the night before His crucifixion. John 16:12ff. applies ONLY to the apostles! Also, passages speaking about how we are "led by the Spirit" are not talking about being led through inward teaching, but by being given inward *strength* (*moral power*) to obey God's will as taught to us in the Bible.

A basic principle is this: the indwelling Holy Spirit does not act upon our *intellect*; He acts upon our *will*. Romans 8:14, says, "For all who are being led by the Spirit of God, these are sons of God." Please read this in context! Verse 13 says, "For if you are living according to the flesh, you must die; but if by the Spirit you are putting to death the deeds of the body, you will live." The Holy Spirit *leads* us by giving us the power to *flee from sin*! Verse 14 explains verse 13; they are connected by the Greek word *gar*, "for, because." Also, verse 16 does not say that the Holy Spirit testifies TO our spirit, but *along with* our spirit—to the Father.

The danger of relying on any personal experience, including subjective or mystical experiences such as the above, is seen in Matthew 7:21-23. Here Jesus says, "Not everyone who says to Me, 'Lord, Lord,' will enter the kingdom of heaven, but he who does the will of My Father who is in heaven *will enter*. Many will say to Me on that day, 'Lord, Lord, did we not prophesy in Your name, and in Your name cast out demons, and in Your name perform many miracles?' And then I will declare to them, 'I never knew you; DEPART FROM ME, YOU WHO PRACTICE LAWLESSNESS.'"

A preacher-friend of mine sent me an email about a member from another church that he was counseling. The minister of this other church had begun to preach false doctrine about the Holy Spirit, a false view of baptism in the Spirit, and false expectations about the Spirit. This church member was deeply disturbed about this, and sent my friend the following email (edited; real names not used):

I had a terrible experience yesterday with a deacon from this [other] church. I approached him and wanted to ask him about these things. Before I could even start, he said, "Joe, I know you are concerned, but I have to tell you, I don't want to stop [what our preacher is] preaching. Something good is happening here. I have to tell you what happened to me."

He proceeded to tell me he was so shaken, he went to a room up front in our church and fell on his knees and was baptized in the Holy Spirit. He said "I don't know how but the Holy Spirit took over my body and hasn't left." He said on three occasions the Holy Spirit has told him what to say and how to act. He says the Holy Spirit told him to sit by me and tell me he was glad I was there. He said, "I know you don't like what our preacher is preaching, but I can see and feel things happening in here." My answer was, "Mike, please read this book I want to study with you on this subject." He said, "I don't need to read it. I have the Holy Spirit in me, telling me what to do next, leading me. I love you, Joe, but I see good things happening here."

I'm sad because I just could not touch the emotional high he was and is having. He was like a drugged person. It seemed nothing I could say would help convince him of anything different from what he was feeling and has been feeling for the last three weeks."

We must constantly be on guard against "voices" somehow coming to us from within ourselves. The Holy Spirit speaks to us through His Word, the Bible.

III. HOW THE HOLY SPIRIT GIVES US POWER

I said in our first session that the Spirit gives three kinds of power: miraculous power, ministering power, and moral power. Here we are dealing with the last one of these.

The name that we usually apply to this particular work of the Spirit is *sanctification*. The Holy Spirit dwells within us to *sanctify* us, literally, to *"make us holy,"* as God is holy (1 Peter 1:15-16). (One kind of sanctification is *initial* sanctification, which is the new Christian's one-time "setting apart" from the world [1 Corinthians 6:11; Colossians 1:13]. We are dealing here with *progressive* sanctification, i.e., the process of growing and maturing in the Christian life, as in 1 Thessalonians 5:23.)

The whole point of the Holy Spirit's work of regeneration in baptism is to prepare us for an ongoing, life-long journey of developing holy character and holy conduct. In that moment He plants within us the seeds of holiness. Then He stays within us to give us strength to walk this path of holiness and to enable the seeds to grow to maturity.

Old Testament saints did not have this inward power; I believe this is one reason God gave them their own land for their dwelling place, to separate and isolate them from the temptations of the pagan world. Christians, however, are commanded to go into all the world. But we need not fear! Ever since Pentecost the Holy Spirit has been within us Christians to give us power to resist temptation and be strong in our wills. He gives us power by strengthening our wills to do what we already know is right. Our biggest problem is not lack of knowledge, but the need for power! See Romans 7:15, 19-20. But that power is already within us, via the indwelling of the Holy Spirit! Thus we can obey Matthew 28:18-20 with confidence!

How does the Bible describe this sanctifying work of the Spirit? Here are some key texts.

- **Ephesians 2:10** says that "we are his workmanship, created in Christ Jesus"—i.e., regenerated by the Holy Spirit—expressly "for good works, which God prepared beforehand, that we should walk in them." The purpose of the regeneration is to enable us to obey God's law commandments for the rest of our lives.

- **Ephesians 3:16** is a prayer by Paul that God "would grant you, according to the riches of His glory, to be strengthened with power through His Spirit in the inner man." This shows us that *power* is the point of the Spirit's indwelling, and that we can access it by prayer.

- **Philippians 2:13** tells us that "it is God who is at work in you, both to will and to work for *His* good pleasure." In view of other Scriptures, we conclude that Paul is speaking here of God the Spirit, who dwells within us and is *working* within us, so that our lives may be pleasing to God.

- **Romans 8:13**, reflecting on the Spirit who indwells us (see vv. 9-11), warns us that as Christians we cannot continue living our old pre-conversion lifestyle. If you do, "you will die," i.e., go back into your old state of spiritual death. "But if by the Spirit you put to death the deeds of the body, you will live"! This shows that it is the power of the indwelling Spirit that enables us to overcome sin in our lives. (See Ephesians 6:12; 1 John 4:4.) The Holy Spirit is steroids for the soul!

- **Galatians 5:22-23** says that Christian virtues such as love, joy, patience, and self-control are the "fruit of the Spirit," i.e., they can be produced in our lives through the indwelling Holy Spirit.

I will remind you again that this is what it means to be LED by the Spirit, as in Romans 8:14 and Galatians 5:18. Sometimes this is called *walking* by the Spirit, as in Galatians 5:16 and Romans 8:4. Also, Galatians 5:25 says that we follow in the steps of the Spirit (*stoicheō*).

This is also what it means to "be filled by the Spirit," as we are commanded to do in Ephesians 5:18. This is a command, an imperative; it is not something we wait for the Holy Spirit to do. Rather, it is our responsibility; it involves our submission and cooperation. It is also a *present* imperative, signifying continuing action. Basically, to be filled with the Spirit means to take full advantage of the already-present and available power of the Spirit residing within us. It means to be more fully submitted to His sanctifying power. It means to *open up all* the rooms in the house in which the Spirit is dwelling (i.e., your body). It means to let the Spirit fill you with good things, such as wisdom, joy, power, peace, and righteousness.

In conclusion, the power to do these things is already within us. Are we using it? (See the next lesson on HOW to use this power.)

Sometimes I wonder what it would have been like if Clark Kent had lived his whole life without knowing he was Superman! I can see him on his deathbed, looking down at his torso, and mumbling, "What's that big "S" on my T-shirt?" This would have been a tragedy! A much greater tragedy is that many Christians have been living their whole lives without knowing and using the power of the Holy Spirit within them. Please – on your deathbed, don't look down and mumble, "What's that big "HS" on my T-shirt?"

PART FIVE:
THE EIGHT-FOLD PATH TO HOLINESS

INTRODUCTION

The Holy Spirit gives us two main kinds of gifts: knowledge and power. The primary gift is knowledge, which He gives by giving us the Bible. The *only* way the Holy Spirit gives us knowledge is through the Bible – *not* via some mystical, inner guidance.

Our concern here, though, is with how the Spirit gives us *power*. We have noted that He gives His people three kinds of power: (1) ministering power, via "spiritual gifts"—which is not our subject here; (2) miraculous power (such as tongues and healing)—which has already been discussed; and (3) moral power, or the power to *be good*. This last one is our topic for now.

As human beings made in God's image, we are under moral obligation to "be good," i.e., to be holy as God is holy (1 Peter 1:15-16), to be perfect as the Father is perfect (Matthew 5:48). This daunting responsibility requires two things: ONE, it requires *knowing* what constitutes goodness, holiness, and perfection. The Holy Spirit gives us this knowledge via Scripture. TWO, it requires *doing* what we know is good. Here is where our main problem lies.

Our problem is the fact that SIN has entered into the world and into our lives, and has affected our very being, our moral nature. It has weakened and distorted our *ability* to be good, our moral power to obey God's will. Our spiritual nature is sinful, spiritually sick, depraved – not totally so, contrary to Calvinism; but depraved and weakened nonetheless. As Jeremiah 17:9 says, "The heart is more deceitful than all else and is desperately sick; who can understand it?" In the words of Paul (Romans 7:15, 19) – "For what I am doing, I do not understand; for I am not practicing what I would like to do, but I am doing the very thing I hate.... For the good that I want, I do not do, but I practice the very evil that I do not want." As sinners we are under the power of sin. As Romans 8:7-8 says, "Because the mind set on the flesh is hostile toward God; for it does not subject itself to the law of God, for it is not even able to do so, and those who are in the flesh cannot please God."

In Romans 7:21-24 Paul utters this heartfelt prayer concerning this captivity to sin: "I find then the principle that evil is present in me, the one who wants to do good. For I joyfully concur with the law of God in the inner man, but I see a different law in the members of my body, waging war against the law of my mind and making me a prisoner of the law of sin which is in my members. Wretched man that I am! Who will set me free from the body of this death?" But then comes his joyful cry of victory in verse 25: "Thanks be to God through Jesus Christ our Lord!"

Then in Romans 8 Paul sets forth the two-fold nature of this victory (the double cure). First, in verses 1-4, he says that we have been set free from the *condemnation* of sin via Christ's atoning sacrifice. The connection between sin and death has been broken. We are living in the state of forgiveness; we do not have to focus our spiritual energy on earning God's forgiveness and pardon.

Paul continues in verses 5-14 to show us that we have also been set free from the *power* of sin by the indwelling Holy Spirit. As I say in my *College Press NIV Commentary on Romans* (first ed., I:458-9), "The indwelling Spirit has broken the power of the indwelling sin which seeks to drag us back down into the pits of spiritual death. When Christ gave us his Spirit, the principle and power of life took over, thus ending the illegitimate reign of those usurping tyrants, sin and death." Also, "The energizing power of the Spirit of life enables us to overcome the insidious power of sin and death that remains in our bodies" (ibid., I:464).

This is what we call *SANCTIFICATION*. The main point is that in our baptism into Christ, God gave us the gift of the indwelling Holy Spirit, for the specific purpose of supplying us with sanctifying power, the power to live a life of obedience to God's law, a life of holiness before the Holy God.

But the question remains: how does this work? The Holy Spirit is in us; His sanctifying power is in us. But how can we ACCESS that power? Is there a switch we can flip, a power cord we can plug in? It's not quite that simple. I have drawn up a plan involving *eight steps*. I call it **THE CHRISTIAN'S EIGHT-FOLD PATH TO HOLINESS THROUGH THE HOLY SPIRIT.**

I want to make it clear that I formulated this 8-step plan *before* I remembered that Buddhism also has something called "The 8-Fold Path," supposedly put together by the founding Buddha, Siddhartha Gautama (b. India, c. 560 B.C.). As a remedy for human ignorance, Buddha set forth his "four noble truths," as follows: (a) Man's basic problem is *suffering*. "To exist is to suffer." (b) The immediate cause of all suffering is *desire*, lust, craving – desire for existence itself, desire for pleasure, desire for prosperity. (c) Such desire can be eradicated by following the *eight-fold path*, which includes *right conduct*. (d) Right conduct includes a list of ten commandments which are intended to be followed by serious Buddhists, especially monks.

The third noble truth says that all desire can be removed by following an eight-fold path, as follows:

1. Right views or knowledge, i.e., enlightenment.
2. Right aspirations or intentions.
3. Right speech.

4.   Right conduct or action. (See below.)

5.   Right livelihood.

6.   Right endeavor or effort.

7.   Right awareness.

8.   Right meditation or concentration.

And just for our information, Buddhism's "right conduct" includes this list of "ten commandments." (Some think the last five apply only to certain holy seasons.)

1.   Not to kill.

2.   Not to steal.

3.   Not to lie.

4.   Not to commit adultery.

5.   Not to drink intoxicants.

6.   Not to eat at forbidden times.

7.   Not to indulge in dancing and theatricals.

8.   Not to use any form of personal adornment.

9.   Not to use a broad or high bed.

10. Not to receive gold or silver.

So — how does this compare with the *Christian's* 8-fold path to holiness? *Any similarities are purely coincidental!!* But the comparison is very interesting at places. And again I remind you that our goal is to explain HOW we Christians may use—or better, how we may allow the Holy Spirit to use—the sanctifying power He has brought into our lives. What follows is an explanation of the eight steps.

I.   INFORMATION

The first step is *information,* or what Buddha calls "right knowledge." Indeed, this is the starting point. But we get our knowledge not from some human being but from the Holy Spirit, specifically, from the objective source that he has provided: the Bible. See Psalms 119:105, "Your word is a lamp to my feet and a light to my path." 2 Timothy 3:16-17 adds, "All Scripture is breathed out by God and is profitable for teaching, for reproof, for correction, for training in righteousness; so that the man of God may be adequate, equipped for every good work." The Bible shows us the path we must walk. It gives us three kinds of necessary information for sanctification. We must *know from Scripture* the following:

- Information about *the ideal Christian life*, or what constitutes *holiness*. What kind of life IS a "holy life"? A preacher-friend once told me that before he was a Christian he thought he would go to heaven as long as he did not commit murder. Well, it's a bit more than this. We have our OWN "10 commandments," and much more. We know that all commandments applicable to this New Covenant age have to be obeyed not just outwardly but inwardly as well.

- Information about *what constitutes sin*. The ideal life is not freedom from suffering, but freedom from SIN. We know what counts as sin from Scripture. This is the negative side of the above.

- Information about *where your own life stands*. This comes via comparison of your life with the Biblical ideal. This requires not only a study of the Bible, but also serious meditation upon its teaching and how our life measures up to it. See Psalms 119:15, 48, 97-104.

II. AWARENESS

The second step in our eight-fold path to holiness is to have a true *awareness* of what the Bible actually teaches about the Holy Spirit, and especially about His work. This includes the following:

- Awareness of the fact THAT the Holy Spirit is within us. We know this not by feeling or experience, but by Scriptures such as the following: Ezekiel 36:25-27; John 7:37-39; Acts 2:38; 1 Corinthians 6:19; Romans 8:9-11; Galatians 4:6; 2 Timothy 1:14. See the reference to "His Spirit in the inner man," Ephesians 3:16.

- Awareness of WHY the Holy Spirit is within us. See again Ephesians 3:16; Philippians 2:12-13; Romans 8:13-14. The emphasis is on *power* to be good.

- Awareness of Ephesians 4:30, which instructs us not to GRIEVE the Holy Spirit of God who is in us. How do we grieve Him? By ignoring and not using the sanctifying power He has already provided us.

III. DESIRE

The third step on the pathway to holiness is *desire*. Buddhism of course is wrong to condemn ALL desire, and to say that desire is the root of all suffering, and that we must get rid of all desire. A key New Testament word is *epithumia*, "strong desire." Sometimes it is bad, sometimes it is good. Some desire is definitely wrong, especially when *epithumia* is translated as "evil desire" or "lust." See, for example, Mark 4:13; 1 John 2:16; Romans 1:24; 6:12; 13:14; Galatians 5:16; and Ephesians 4:22. But, contra Buddhism, some "strong desire" (*epithumia*) is good. In Luke 22:15 Jesus said to his apostles, "I have earnestly desired to eat this Passover with you before I suffer." In Philippians 1:23 Paul declared that he had "the desire (*epithumia*) to depart and be with Christ." He told the Thessalonians that he had a "great desire" to see their faces (1 Thessalonians 2:17).

The key, of course is the *object* of our desire. The issue is not THAT we desire, but WHAT we desire. See Romans 7:19, where Paul says, "For the good that **I want**, I do not do, but I practice the very evil that **I do not**

want." He is lamenting the fact that his deeds are not cooperating with his desires, but he is desiring the right thing: he wants to be good, and to be rid of sin! The desire to be rid of sin is an essential desire; it is at the very heart of repentance. The desire to be *holy* should be constantly with us. In the words of a chorus we used to sing as children, "My desire—to be like Jesus; my desire—to be like Him! His Spirit fill me; His love o'erwhelm me! In deed and word, to be like Him."

IV. PRAYER

Step four is prayer, and here is where we begin to personally and directly plug into the power source provided for us by the indwelling Holy Spirit, the *power for holy living* that already exists within us. We begin to access it by prayer.

Ephesians 3:16 is a model for this; it is Paul's PRAYER for Christians everywhere. He prays that God "would grant you, according to the riches of His glory, to be strengthened with power through His Spirit in the inner man." We should make this our own prayer for ourselves, with one major modification, namely, by making it *specific*. Ephesians 3:16 is very general, but we can and should make it more specific than this. We must pray *specifically* for the Spirit's power to aid us in overcoming SPECIFIC sins. Our prayer should not be just, "I pray that the Holy Spirit will help me to grow as a Christian and resist temptation." It should be rather: "I pray that the Holy Spirit will give me the power to overcome my anger/lust/laziness/foul language" – fill in the blank with whatever sins are present in your life.

As we can see, this kind of prayer involves the confession of sins. It also goes hand in hand with the previous step (desire). I.e., one of the main prayers we must utter is that the Spirit would help us to *desire* to be rid of specific sins. See Philippians 2:13 again: "For it is God who is at work in you, both to will [i.e., *desire*] and to work for His good pleasure." Such prayer often must be strenuous, fervent, persistent, and lengthy (measured in hours).

V.   SURRENDER

The next step involves an attitude of sincere surrender to the power and purpose of the Holy Spirit and His presence within us. Though our own effort is involved in this eight-step process, it is vital what we realize that our own will power is simply not sufficient to take us to our goal of holiness. See Romans 7:14ff. again, where Paul confesses his personal weakness in the face of temptation, and his need for help from outside himself. This step is basically a confession of our own weakness and helplessness by ourselves. It is an act of yielding to the power of the Holy Spirit, and granting that we are dependent upon him.

This is especially important in view of Ephesians 6:10ff., where we are exhorted to "put on the full armor of God" in view of the fact that we are facing a horde of spiritual enemies led by Satan himself. We must realize that Satan and his demons are working against us, tempting us and leading us into sin. We also understand that some sins are intensified by demonic presence within us, which makes them more difficult to overcome. Luther certainly had it right: "Did we in our own strength confide, our striving would be losing. Were not the right one on our side— the one of God's own choosing." We confess that we need a power stronger than our own. And the fact is that we DO have this stronger power: "Greater is He who is in you than he who is in the world"! (1 John 4:4).

VI.   TRUST

The next step is to *trust* all of God's promises regarding the Spirit's presence and purpose within us. Here we acknowledge that we were not directly conscious of the Spirit's entry into our bodies at our baptism, nor are we consciously aware of his continuing presence therein. We do not experience objective sensations that confirm these realities. All of this is simply a matter of faith: we trust God's Word of promise that He has given us the Holy Spirit in our baptism, and that the Spirit is still within us and is helping us to be holy. Even as we pray, we must have faith that the Spirit will really provide the needed power for which we are praying. This helps us to understand Acts 26:18 when it says that we are "sanctified by faith." We know from experience that we cannot trust in ourselves; we can only lean on the Spirit for our needed moral strength.

VII. ACTION

The seventh step is *action*, by which we mean that we must be making every personal attempt to involve ourselves in this quest for holiness. Here we must acknowledge that sanctification is not a process in which we are simply passive robots. This is not like the event of regeneration which began this process. That was completely the work of the Holy Spirit; we were simply submitting to his working as we submit to a surgeon on the operating table. Sanctification, though, is rather like the follow-up recovery period, where we must follow the doctor's instructions and invest our own effort into the process (exercise, diet, rest). We must ACT.

This is simply acknowledging that we are by nature *free-will beings*. We must make the decisions and make the effort to resist temptation and to do right, while leaning on the power of the Spirit to help us follow through with our intentions, desires, and efforts. Thus we do not expect the Holy Spirit to actually take possession of our bodies, in some sense like demon possession. We maintain control, and we must act – but only after we have absorbed steps 1 through 6 above!

See the connection between Philippians 2:12 and 2:13. We are told in verse 12 to work out the sanctification aspect of our own salvation with "fear and trembling." As the first word in verse 13 shows ("for"), the reason for the fear and trembling is not the fear of terror but the fear of reverential awe at the fact that *God Himself*, in the person of the Holy Spirit, is dwelling in us and giving us the power to *want* to do what is right as well as to actually *do* it. The point, though, is that we must make the conscious effort to seriously work at growing in holiness.

VIII. THANKSGIVING

The last step may be the easiest to do, but also the easiest to forget. I.e., we must remember to *thank God* for his gift of the Holy Spirit, and to give the Holy Spirit Himself the praise and credit for every victory over sin that we experience. This will help us to avoid spiritual pride. To GOD be the glory!

SECTION TWO

MISCELLANEOUS STUDIES ON THE HOLY SPIRIT

THE PROMISE OF THE FATHER
ACTS 1:4-5

This is my latest composition on the Holy Spirit. I prepared it in the summer of 2018 for presentation at the Christian Restoration Association's 2018 Bible Conference, held in Mason, OH, on October 18-19. The theme of the conference was "Acts in Action." Those invited to speak were told to select any passage of their choice from the Book of Acts as the basis for their message. I was happy to accept the invitation and, beginning with Acts 1:4-5, to speak on the various ways the Holy Spirit is described as working in the early church.

I wanted to speak on this subject because, judging from the many questions that come to me about this, there is a lot of confusion about it. So I chose Jesus's reference to "what the Father had promised," mentioned in Acts 1:4-5. I am hoping that this exposition can help clear up two serious misunderstandings: (1) the application of "baptism in the Holy Spirit" to Acts 2:1-13 instead of Acts 2:38-39; and (2) the idea that Acts 8 and Acts 10 prove that baptism is not for salvation. Both of these conclusions are wrong, and my explanation of "the promise of the Father" will show why.

There may be some overlapping with one or two of the other entries here, but I wanted to include this since it is my most recent work on the subject. Biblical quotations are from the NASB or ESV, unless otherwise noted.

INTRODUCTION

How does the Book of Acts fit into the broad scope of salvation history? It is a critical historical record, because it records what is truly one of the most momentous turning points in all of world history—not just salvation history. I am speaking of the Day of Pentecost as recorded in

Acts 2. As a pivotal point in history, Pentecost is overshadowed only by the redemptive work of Jesus's death and resurrection. This is certainly true from the standpoint of the way we live our lives every day.

What is so significant about Pentecost? Here are five pivotal *new things* that began on that day:

- God inaugurated a new kind of special people: THE CHURCH.
- God began a new way of relating to His people: the NEW COVENANT.
- God began to require a new, expanded version of saving faith: faith in THE TRINITY.
- God ordained a new condition for receiving salvation: CHRISTIAN BAPTISM.
- God began to include a new aspect in the gift of salvation: the INDWELLING HOLY SPIRIT.

Many false doctrines and theological problems are the result of a failure to understand these monumental changes. My focus here is on the last of the above five points: the new gift of the Holy Spirit. This is the point of my Scripture text, Acts 1:4-5 (NASB): "Gathering them together, He commanded them not to leave Jerusalem, but to wait for what the Father had promised, 'Which,' He said, 'you heard of from Me; for John baptized with water, but you will be baptized with the Holy Spirit not many days from now.'"

I plan to address two main theological issues that can be resolved by coming to a proper understanding of this text, as it focuses on "the promise of the Father," that promise being the imminent *baptism in the Holy Spirit*. What are these two issues?

The first issue is what I will call the Zwinglian problem (also known as the faith-only problem). The issue is whether baptism in water is a salvation event. Most of the Protestant world denies it; and ironically they like to use the Book of Acts as proof of this denial—especially by referring to what is said about the Holy Spirit in Acts 8 and Acts 10-11. The second issue is the common Restoration Movement tendency to limit what is called the "baptism in the Holy Spirit" to two main events in the Book of Acts, i.e., the miraculous gifts of tongue-speaking in Acts 2:1-13 (Pentecost) and Acts 10:44-48 (Cornelius).

The key to resolving these two issues, and correcting the errors related thereto, is a right understanding of "the promise of the Father" in Acts 1:4-5 (and Acts 2:33).

I.   FOUR KINDS OF GIFTS GIVEN BY THE HOLY SPIRIT

I am convinced that in this New Covenant age salvation begins in the moment of Christian baptism, and I am convinced that this moment is the time when the seeking sinner receives the saving gift of the Holy Spirit. This saving presence of the Spirit is a mark of salvation (Ephesians 1:13).

However, most modern Protestantism follows Huldreich Zwingli's repudiation of any connection between baptism and salvation. They believe that salvation, including the gift of the indwelling Spirit, is given at the moment one begins to believe in Jesus. One of their most common arguments is that the Book of Acts shows that there is *no appointed connection* between baptism and the receiving of the Spirit; see especially the Samaritan converts in Acts 8:12-17 and Cornelius and his household in Acts 10:44-48.

Our response to this fallacious argument is to point out that there are four different ways in which the Holy Spirit is given and received, or (to say it another way) four kinds of gifts given by the Holy Spirit—only one of which is connected with salvation. Once we understand this, we will see that the Zwinglian argument from the Book of Acts is completely false. This is because those who use it, fail to properly distinguish among these four different purposes for receiving the presence of the Holy Spirit.

SECTION TWO: MISCELLANEOUS STUDIES ON
THE HOLY SPIRIT

Here we will proceed to describe these four ways of relating to the Holy Spirit. First we should note that as long as God has had a "special people," the Holy Spirit has worked among, within, and through them in several different ways. This applies to both Old Testament Israel and the New Testament Church. Three kinds of the Spirit's works were present under the Old Covenant, and four kinds are present today.

Here is one caution, before we go any further. One cannot distinguish these four kinds of Spirit-presence by the *language* used to describe them. Many different verbal formulas are used interchangeably in Scripture to describe these different kinds of working of the Spirit. For example:

- The Spirit is given, and the Spirit gives gifts.
- The Spirit is a gift, and the Spirit is received.
- The Spirit is poured out on someone, and the Spirit comes upon someone.
- The Spirit falls upon someone, and one is filled with the Spirit.
- The Spirit dwells within someone, and the Spirit rests upon someone.
- One is baptized in the Spirit, and one drinks of the Spirit.
- One is led by the Spirit, and one is strengthened by the Spirit.

Nothing is implied by these various pairings. The point is that there are many ways in which the Spirit is described as "being given to" or as "giving something to" an individual, and the language by itself cannot be the determining factor as to which kind of gift is intended.

Here I will name and describe the different ways the Holy Spirit connects with individuals in order to GIVE him or her something. I will show that there are *four different kinds* of "somethings," described here as "gifts." These four specific kinds of gifts bestowed by the Spirit are four distinct ways the Spirit works in and through individuals.

First, the Spirit gives TRUTH gifts. These are powers and abilities that involve revelation and inspiration, whereby chosen individuals are enabled to speak or write God-breathed messages from God to mankind. David the psalmist says in 2 Samuel 23:2, "The Spirit of the LORD spoke by me, and His word was on my tongue." 2 Peter 1:21 affirms it thus: "For no prophecy was ever made by an act of human will, but men moved by the Holy Spirit spoke from God."

The second kind of gift is SIGN gifts. These are the ability to perform *miracles* of all sorts, for the specific purpose of giving evidence or proof of the divine origin of accompanying revelation or inspired messages (i.e., truth gifts). One of the New Testament's oft-used names for miracles is *signs*. Here is how Paul puts it in 2 Corinthians 12:12, "The signs of a true apostle were performed among you with all perseverance, by signs and wonders and miracles." Many of these are named in 1 Corinthians 12:9-11 and attributed to the Holy Spirit. An Old Testament example is an event similar to Pentecost, described in Numbers 11:16-30. When Moses needed help in managing the people of Israel, it was decided that seventy men would be chosen to receive the Holy Spirit's service gift of leadership (see the next paragraph). When the Spirit came upon them for this purpose, He also gave them the *sign* gift of miraculous speaking (called *prophesying*). See verses 25-26:

> Then the LORD came down in the cloud and spoke to him [Moses]; and He took of the Spirit who was upon him and placed Him upon the seventy elders. And when the Spirit rested upon them, they prophesied. But they did not do it again. But two men had remained in the camp; the name of one was Eldad and the name of the other Medad. And the Spirit rested upon them (now they were among those who had been registered, but had not gone out to the tent), and they prophesied in the camp.

The third kind of gift bestowed by the Spirit upon individuals is SERVICE gifts. The previous two gifts also enable the recipient to serve God in different ways, but I am reserving this term for the ordinary (i.e., non-miraculous) tasks and abilities bestowed on individuals to enable them to *serve* the people of God in specific ways, i.e., to meet the various needs for the well-being of the people of God. The distinguishing point here is that these gifts do not involve miraculous or supernatural powers for the purpose of receiving and verifying inspired messages from God. The seventy elders in Numbers 11:16-30 received both kinds of gifts— both a sign gift and a service gift. The sign gift was given simply to prove or verify that God was bestowing the service gift upon them also. For other such service gifts in the Old Testament, see Exodus 31:1-11, and 1 Samuel 16:13. In the New Testament several are named in Romans 12:7-8.

References to such service gifts from the Holy Spirit are mostly absent from the narrative in the Book of Acts, so they will not figure into our discussion below. (One place such a gift might appear is Acts 6:3.)

Finally, the fourth kind of gift is SALVATION gifts. This one was not present in the Old Covenant era; it began on Pentecost. In this gift the Holy Spirit becomes present in the body, spirit, and life of sinners who have obeyed the gospel, in order to bestow upon them the saving gifts of regeneration and sanctification. This is the "new birth" by the Spirit of which John 3:5 speaks. See how Titus 3:5 describes it: "He saved us, not on the basis of deeds which we have done in righteousness, but according to His mercy, by the washing of regeneration and renewing by the Holy Spirit."

In the Book of Acts it is critically important to distinguish among the *truth* gifts, the *sign* gifts, and the *salvation* gifts. These are not necessarily given as a package, and are not necessarily given in a particular order. Here are important examples of this:

In Acts 2, (i) the *sign* gift comes first, namely, the speaking in tongues, vv. 4-13. It is given to verify what follows. (ii) The *truth* gift is what follows; this is Peter's sermon, vv. 14ff. This is spoken through the Spirit's inspiration, as Jesus promised in John 16:12-15. This is given to explain this whole Pentecostal event, and especially that which follows. (iii) What follows is the *salvation* gift, which is the climactic point. The Spirit gives the salvation gift in baptism, vv. 38-39.

In Acts 10, (i) the truth gift comes first, i.e., Peter's sermon in vv. 34ff. (ii) The sign gift follows, to prove the truth of Peter's message. The sign is the gift of speaking in tongues, vv. 44ff. (iii) Finally comes the salvation gift, which is the climactic point. It is again given in baptism, vv. 47-48.

In Acts 8:4-13, (i) the truth gift is Philip's preaching, vv. 4-5. (ii) Then come the sign gifts, i.e., Philip's miracles, vv. 6-8. (iii) We conclude that the salvation gift is given in baptism, vv. 12-13. This conclusion is justified in view of Acts 5:32, where Peter and the other apostles refer to "the Holy Spirit, whom God has given to those who obey Him." This is a reference to obeying the gospel, which the Samaritans did when they were baptized by Philip.

In Acts 8:14-24, the issue is the giving of truth and sign gifts ONLY. Though many Samaritans were baptized and had received the salvation gift, none as yet had received any of the truth and sign gifts. This is why apostles came to them from Jerusalem, because such truth and sign gifts could be bestowed via the laying on of the apostles' hands (Acts 6:6; 8:17; 19:6). Simon's reaction to the result of the laying on of hands shows that this result was sign gifts, not the salvation gift (Acts 8:18ff.).

The Zwinglian error is to assume that every reference to the coming (or giving) of the Holy Spirit upon someone must be a salvation event. This is simply NOT TRUE. It is an example of extremely faulty interpretation of the Bible, in the interests of supporting a false doctrine.

II. THE NEW WAY THE SPIRIT BEGINS TO WORK ON PENTECOST

One clear theme of predictive prophecy is that for many centuries God was planning to *do something new* among His people through a special working of the Holy Spirit. This theme appears in several Old Testament prophets and in the preaching of John the Baptist and Jesus as recorded in the New Testament. It becomes clear that this "new thing" will happen on the Day of Pentecost.

Many Christians, especially including Pentecostals but also including many in the Restoration Movement, have identified the fulfillment of this prophecy to be a kind of SIGN GIFT, i.e., the Pentecostal gift of speaking in tongues. This is associated with the promise of baptism in the Holy Spirit; this promise is seen as being fulfilled in the gift of tongues especially.

I believe this is a seriously faulty interpretation of the prophecies and promises of a new working of the Holy Spirit, and a seriously wrong analysis of the data given in the Book of Acts. Here I will show that "the promise of the Father" of a new working of the Spirit—described by John the Baptist and Jesus as "baptism in the Holy Spirit"—is the SALVATION gift of the indwelling of the Spirit.

This promise of the Father was first verbalized in several Old Testament prophecies, then emphasized by both John the Baptist and Jesus. Pentecost was the fulfillment of a whole string of such prophecies and promises that say the Holy Spirit is going to do something NEW. This newness is a crucial point in identifying the fulfillment of this promise. Where do we find this "promise of the Father"?

Isaiah 43:19-21; 44:3-4. [19] "Behold, **I will do something new**, now it will spring forth; will you not be aware of it? I will even make a roadway in the wilderness, rivers in the desert. [20] The beasts of the field will glorify Me, the jackals and the ostriches, because I have given waters in the wilderness and rivers in the desert, to give drink to My chosen people. [21] The people whom I formed for Myself Will declare My praise.... [3] For I will pour out water on the thirsty *land* and streams on the dry ground; I will pour out My Spirit on your offspring and My blessing on your descendants; [4] And they will spring up among the grass like poplars by streams of water."

Ezekiel 36:25-27. [25] "Then I will sprinkle clean water on you, and you will be clean; I will cleanse you from all your filthiness and from all your idols. [26] Moreover, I will give you a new heart and put a new spirit within you; and I will remove the heart of stone from your flesh and give you a heart of flesh. [27] I will put My Spirit within you and cause you to walk in My statutes, and you will be careful to observe My ordinances."

Joel 2:28-32a. [28] "It will come about after this that I will pour out My Spirit on all mankind; And your sons and daughters will prophesy, your old men will dream dreams, your young men will see visions. [29] Even on the male and female servants I will pour out My Spirit in those days. [30] I will display wonders in the sky and on the earth, blood, fire and columns of smoke. [31] The sun will be turned into darkness and the moon into blood before the great and awesome day of the LORD comes. [32] And it will come about that whoever calls on the name of the LORD will be delivered."

Matthew 3:11. "As for me, I baptize you with water for repentance, but He who is coming after me is mightier than I, and I am not fit to remove His sandals; He will baptize you with the Holy Spirit and fire." (See Luke 3:16 also.)

John 1:32-34. [32] John testified saying, "I have seen the Spirit descending as a dove out of heaven, and He remained upon Him. [33] I did not recognize Him, but He who sent me to baptize in water said to me, 'He upon whom you see the Spirit descending and remaining upon Him, this is the One who baptizes in the Holy Spirit.' [34] I myself have seen, and have testified that this is the Son of God."

John 4:7-14. [7] There came a woman of Samaria to draw water. Jesus said to her, "Give Me a drink." [8] For His disciples had gone away into the city to buy food. [9] Therefore the Samaritan woman said to Him, "How is it that You, being a Jew, ask me for a drink since I am a Samaritan woman?" (For Jews have no dealings with Samaritans.) [10] Jesus answered and said to her, "If you knew the gift of God, and who it is who says to you, 'Give Me a drink,' you would have asked Him, and He would have given you living water." [11] She said to Him, "Sir, You have nothing to draw with and the well is deep; where then do You get that living water? [12] You are not greater than our father Jacob, are You, who gave us the well, and drank of it himself and his sons and his cattle?" [13] Jesus answered and said to her, "Everyone who drinks of this water will thirst again; [14] but whoever drinks of the water that I will give him shall never thirst; but the water that I will give him will become in him a well of water springing up to eternal life."

John 7:37-39. [37] Now on the last day, the great *day* of the feast, Jesus stood and cried out, saying, "If anyone is thirsty, let him come to Me and drink. [38] He who believes in Me, as the Scripture said, 'From his innermost being will flow rivers of living water.'" [39] But this He spoke of the Spirit, whom those who believed in Him were to receive; for the Spirit was not yet *given*, because Jesus was not yet glorified.

Luke 24:45-49. [45] Then He opened their minds to understand the Scriptures, [46] and He said to them, "Thus it is written, that the Christ would suffer and rise again from the dead the third day, [47] and that repentance for forgiveness of sins would be proclaimed in His name to all the nations, beginning from Jerusalem. [48] You are witnesses of these things. [49] And behold, I am sending forth the promise of My Father upon you; but you are to stay in the city until you are clothed with power from on high."

Acts 1:4-8. [4] Gathering them together, He commanded them not to leave Jerusalem, but to wait for what the Father had promised, "Which," *He said*, "you heard of from Me; [5] for John baptized with water, but you will be baptized with the Holy Spirit not many days from now." [6] So when they had come together, they were asking Him, saying, "Lord, is it at this time You are restoring the kingdom to Israel?" [7] He said to them, "It is not for you to know times or epochs which the Father has fixed by His own authority; [8] but you will receive power when the Holy Spirit has come upon you; and you shall be My witnesses both in Jerusalem, and in all Judea and Samaria, and even to the remotest part of the earth."

Acts 2:33. "Therefore having been exalted to the right hand of God, and having received from the Father the promise of the Holy Spirit, He has poured forth this which you both see and hear."

(It is important to understand that all of these prophecies and promises are pointing ahead to the same event—the giving of "the promise of the Father." NOTE: I have not included Jesus's promises of the Spirit in John 14:26; 15:26; and 16:12-15 here because these were given specifically to the apostles and all refer only to the Spirit's *truth* gift, which does not qualify as something new.)

Based on these Scriptures, what are the various aspects of this "promise of the Father"?

1. It is a promise made by God the Father. See the John 1, Luke 24, and Acts 2 selections above.

2. It has to do with a working of the Holy Spirit. See all, above.

3. This work is something remedial—something that corrects a bad situation, described figuratively as dry ground or thirst. See the Isaiah 43, John 4, and John 7 selections above.

4. This is given in abundance; it is like water "poured out" to produce rivers deep enough to be immersed in. See the Isaiah 43, John 1, and Matthew 3 selections.

5. It will not be just a one-time thing, but will continue into future generations. See Isaiah 43 and Joel 2.

6. It will be for all mankind—Gentiles as well as Jews. See Joel 2 and Luke 24.

7. The Spirit will be sent by the Messiah after his resurrection and ascension. See Matthew 3, John 1, John 4, John 7, and Acts 2.

8. This giving of the Spirit will be accompanied by mighty signs and wonders. See Joel 2.

9. This giving of the Spirit is for salvation. See Ezekiel 36, Joel 2, and John 4.

10. This will be given to believers only. See John 7.

11. This will be SOMETHING NEW. See Isaiah 43.

Considering the four ways the Spirit connects with individuals (as explained above), which one of these fits the above criteria? Obviously, only one: the SALVATION GIFT. We should know this from the beginning, because this is the only one that is a *new* way of the Spirit's working. All of the other three are already present prior to Pentecost, in Old Testament times, especially the SIGN gifts (including supernatural speaking [prophesying] as a *sign* of another distinct working of the Spirit—Numbers 11). The saving indwelling presence of the Spirit was not given prior to Pentecost; it was a *new thing* on the Day of Pentecost. This in itself refutes the interpretation of "baptism in the Holy Spirit" as being fulfilled in the gift of tongues on Pentecost, and in any other such sign gifts.

Another consideration that rules out truth and sign gifts as "the promise of the Father" is the fact that this promised gift would be for all who believe and call upon Jesus as Lord, even into future generations. How can we think that something so lavishly promised could be fulfilled in just a few people in just a small number of events (especially just two)? Limiting the baptism in the Spirit to Pentecost and Cornelius just does not live up to the expectations generated by the above string of prophecies! It would be quite disappointing—much ado about very little. The very foundation of all Pentecostal-type denominations and churches is erroneous from the beginning, i.e., thinking that a sign gift could be the main point of Pentecost. The only gift given by the Spirit on Pentecost that can qualify as "the promise of the Father" is the salvation gift.

The following is a summary of what was happening on Pentecost as described in Acts 2.

First is the *outpouring* of the Spirit, in a single event described in vv. 1-3. At this one point of time, Jesus the risen Lord was pouring out the Spirit into a specific physical location in this visible universe (see v. 33). This is when the Spirit Himself was GIVEN; the Spirit then became the Father's gift, being now present and available in that place. ("The gift of the Holy Spirit" in Acts 2:38 may be referring to that already-occurred act of *giving* the Spirit from heaven into this world. Once that has happened, this divine Gift is now ready to enter into anyone who will receive Him by obeying the gospel: "Repent and be baptized, and you will receive the literal presence within yourself of the Holy Spirit, who was just given as the Father's gift for us all!")

The next event, beginning in v. 4 (through v. 13), is the giving of the temporary but extremely conspicuous sign gift: the ability to speak in unlearned foreign languages. This was probably given just to the apostles. This was not a truth gift, in the sense that it was not given for the purpose of communicating some new message from God. The only function of the tongues was to be a miraculous sign to confirm the divine origin and truth of the sermon Peter was about to preach. Once that purpose was accomplished (see vv. 7, 12), there was no further need for this sign gift. (NOTE: the gift of tongues was NOT given as a means of communicating the gospel to the various linguistic groups present. The hearers' response was amazement [vv. 6, 12], not conviction, which is the whole point of sign gifts. Also, there was no need for tongues for this purpose, since Greek was a common language shared by all. Peter's message was heard by all.)

The next great thing on Pentecost was this very truth gift displayed by the Apostle Peter: the preaching of his sermon, vv. 14ff. This is not specifically said, but it is obvious that he was filled with the Spirit's gift of revelation and inspiration. (This was a fulfillment of Jesus's promise specifically to the apostles in John 14:26; 15:26; and 16:12-15.) Why was Peter's sermon so readily accepted by the audience? Because of the *sign gift* that set it up! (Remember—neither such a thing as a sign gift nor a truth gift was something *new*. These were NOT the fulfillment of the promise of the Father.)

Finally comes the main point of Pentecost: the salvation gift itself, vv. 37-39. "You shall receive the gift of the Holy Spirit." How was the audience supposed to know what this meant? How were they to understand it? *In the light of verse 33*, which refers to "the promise of the Holy Spirit" which Jesus had just poured out. The "gift of the Holy Spirit" being offered to Peter's audience is what Jesus had already poured out, as recorded in vv. 1-3, when the *gift* was first given for the church. ("Gift" of the Spirit is not a technical or exclusive term used just for the salvific implanting of the Spirit in the believer in the moment of baptism. See Acts 10:45, where the same terminology is used for a sign gift.)

By introducing the requirement for water baptism as the time for receiving Spirit baptism, the Apostle Peter is describing the fulfillment of the promise specifically of our baptism in the Spirit. Since there is only one baptism (Ephesians 4:5), the water and the Spirit are being joined together here for the first time (a la John 3:5). John the Baptist's disciples were baptized with water only, but Christians are those who have been baptized with BOTH water AND Spirit. See 1 Corinthians 12:13, which says that "by one Spirit we were all baptized into one body." This cannot be a separate event from water baptism, because of Ephesians 4:5.

What is Peter asking his audience to do? He is saying to them, "Repent, and *every one* of you be baptized, and *you too* shall receive the outpoured gift of the Holy Spirit, the very Spirit who was working in that event of tongue-speaking that just amazed you! The now-present Spirit was not just for the Apostles; He is here for YOU also!" See how Titus 3:5-6 uses the same word for "poured out" (*ekcheō*) to describe our individual receiving of the Spirit in baptism, that was used for the initial outpouring in Acts 2:1-3 (see Acts 2:17, 18, 33).

This is seen especially in verse 39, where Peter puts "you" in the first, emphatic position in the sentence: "Because, FOR YOU is the promise!" It's *for you*, not just for the Apostles! And what promise is Peter talking about? The one he has already highlighted in verse 33 and identified in verse 38: "the promise of the Holy Spirit"—whose presence you have already observed in this very place! This promise of the Father is for you! (See again Luke 24:49; Acts 1:4.)

But notice how Peter makes it clear that this promise of the Spirit is not JUST for those present in that audience, who had the privilege of observing the first moments of the fulfilling of this great promise just because they happened to be there on the Day of Pentecost. No, this same promise is for your descendants—future generations! And this promise is for all who are "far off" (Greek, *makran*)—a word used to describe the Gentiles in Ephesians 2:13, 17 (see Acts 22:21).

What we have just described here is the fulfillment of all the prophecies and promises from Isaiah 43 and following, including the promise that Jesus would baptize us in the Holy Spirit. This includes the thousands who were baptized on Pentecost: when they were baptized in water, Jesus was baptizing them in the Holy Spirit!

Does this mean that the thousands who were baptized in water and Spirit on Pentecost immediately began to speak in tongues and do other miraculous things? Absolutely not. This is one of the biggest misunderstandings of baptism in the Spirit, i.e., that it is supposed to convey miracle-working ability of some kind. No, it is a SALVATION gift of the Spirit, not a SIGN gift! In fact, the Book of Acts specifies that after the thousands were baptized on Pentecost, "everyone kept feeling a sense of awe; and many wonders and signs were taking place **through the apostles**" (2:43). The absence of any reference to miracles being done by the early Christians continues through Acts 5:12, where it is said that "at the hands **of the apostles** many signs and wonders were taking place among the people." These thousands of new converts were receiving the salvation gift of the Spirit, but not sign gifts. (The first non-Apostles to work miracles were those upon whom Apostles laid their hands, in part for this very purpose. See Acts 6:6-8; 8:6-8, 18; 19:6. Please understand: Sign gifts from the Holy Spirit *were not the promise of the Father* that was fulfilled for the first time on the Day of Pentecost!)

THE DEITY OF THE HOLY SPIRIT

QUESTION: Who is the Holy Spirit? How is He related to the Father and the Son? Is the Holy Spirit a divine person, one of the three persons of the Trinity?

ANSWER: I have addressed this issue in chapter one of my larger book on the Holy Spirit, *Power from on High: What the Bible Says About the Holy Spirit* (College Press, 2007). This chapter is called "The Person of the Holy Spirit." In it I establish three basic facts. According to the Bible, (1) the Holy Spirit is a *person* in the full and true sense of the word; (2) He is a *divine* person who is to be worshiped; and (3) He is a *distinct* divine person, one of three distinct persons of whom the Trinity is composed.

This essay gives what I have written on the second fact, that the Holy Spirit is a DIVINE person (see pp. 36-40 in the book). The Spirit's deity is manifested by the following lines of biblical evidence.

I.   TRINITARIAN STATEMENTS IN THE NEW TESTAMENT

Several New Testament texts refer to the Father, the Son, and the Spirit in ways that support their unity and equality and thus the deity of the Holy Spirit. The best known and most commonly used text is Matthew 28:19, "Go therefore and make disciples of all the nations, baptizing them in the name of the Father and the Son and the Holy Spirit." The one name unites the three persons. The phrase "into the name of" can mean generally "into a relationship with," which in this context would be a saving relationship in which all three persons of the Trinity participate. In the Greek world the phrase was used specifically as an accounting term for the entry of an item into the list of one's owned assets. Thus the phrase means that in accepting God's salvation a person becomes the "property" equally of the Father, the Son, and the Spirit, and surrenders to their shared lordship. This is difficult to understand if the Spirit is not divine in the same way as the Father and the Son are divine.

Another trinitarian text is the blessing of 2 Corinthians 13:14, "The grace of the Lord Jesus Christ, and the love of God, and the fellowship of the Holy Spirit, be with you." This expresses our continuing dependence on all three persons.

Another text that parallels the three is 1 Corinthians 12:4-6, "Now there are varieties of gifts, but the same Spirit. And there are varieties of ministries, and the same Lord. There are varieties of effects, but the same God who works all things in all persons." Here all three persons of the Trinity are equally involved in the bestowing of what we call "spiritual gifts."

These three texts together show that there is no one proper order for listing the Father, the Son, and the Spirit. We usually use this order because of the influence of the baptismal text, and as a result we usually speak of the Holy Spirit as "the third person of the Trinity." In view of these last two texts, however, we can see that this order is more traditional than normative. As we can see, in 1 Corinthians 12:4-6 the Spirit is actually mentioned first; and in the three texts God (the Father) is placed in all three positions.

Other trinitarian texts include Ephesians 4:4-6, where "one Spirit," "one Lord," and "one God and Father" are each included in the seven basic doctrines that unite believers. Also relevant are 2 Corinthians 1:21-22,

"Now He who establishes us with you in Christ and anointed us is God, who also sealed us and gave us the Spirit in our hearts as a pledge"; and 1 Peter 1:2, which says we are chosen "according to the foreknowledge of God the Father, by the sanctifying work of the Spirit, to obey Jesus Christ and be sprinkled with His blood." These latter two texts again involve all three persons of the Trinity in the work of salvation.

One text that should not be cited to support the Trinity and therefore the deity of the Spirit is 1 John 5:7 in the KJV, "For there are three that bear record in heaven, the Father, the Word, and the Holy Ghost: and these three are one" (see also the NKJV). Most modern translations omit this verse because it is a clear case of a very late addition to the text of the Bible; it is present in no early or even moderately early Greek manuscripts of the New Testament.

II.   THE HOLY SPIRIT HAS DIVINE ATTRIBUTES

Another biblical basis for affirming the Spirit's deity is the fact that He is said to possess divine attributes. Hebrews 9:14 speaks of Him as "the eternal Spirit." According to 1 Timothy 6:16, only God "possesses immortality," i.e., is inherently eternal (see Psalms 90:2).

Also, 1 Corinthians 2:10-11 presents the Holy Spirit as omniscient or all-knowing, since the content of His mind is the same as the content of the Father's mind: "For the Spirit searches all things, even the depths of God. For who among men knows the thoughts of a man except the spirit of the man which is in him? Even so the thoughts of God no one knows except the Spirit of God." Isaiah 40:13-14 suggests that "the Spirit of the LORD" by nature knows all there is to know: "Who has directed the Spirit of the LORD, or as His counselor has informed Him? With whom did He consult and who gave Him understanding? And who taught Him in the path of justice and taught Him knowledge and informed Him of the way of understanding?"

Psalms 139:7-10 clearly involves the Spirit of God in divine omnipresence: "Where can I go from Your Spirit? Or where can I flee from Your presence? If I ascend to heaven, You are there; if I make my bed in Sheol, behold, You are there. If I take the wings of the dawn, if I dwell in the remotest part of the sea, even there Your hand will lead me, and Your right hand will lay hold of me." Also, the fact that the Holy Spirit simultaneously indwells all immersed believers worldwide shows that His essence is not limited by space, which is the very presupposition of omnipresence. (His indwelling is more than His omnipresence, however.)

Though the Bible does not explicitly attribute omnipotence to the Spirit, it does say that he performs works of such great power that we normally think of them as things that only God can do. A main example is creation (Genesis 1:2; Psalms 104:30); another is raising the dead (Romans 8:11). Creation and resurrection are the two masterworks in God's repertoire of omnipotence (Romans 4:17), and the Spirit does both. He is the Spirit of power (Micah 3:8; Zechariah 4:6; Acts 1:8; Romans 15:13, 19).

III. BLASPHEMY AGAINST THE SPIRIT

Jesus teaches that the worst sin anyone can commit is blasphemy against the Holy Spirit, since it is the only sin that "never has forgiveness" (Mark 3:29). His full statement is thus: "Therefore I say to you, any sin and blasphemy shall be forgiven people, but blasphemy against the Spirit shall not be forgiven. Whoever speaks a word against the Son of Man, it shall be forgiven him; but whoever speaks against the Holy Spirit, it shall not be forgiven him, either in this age or in the age to come" (Matthew 12:31-32; see Luke 12:10). This is incomprehensible if the Holy Spirit is not divine, since blasphemy against the Son of Man—Jesus, God the

Son—can be forgiven. Surely blasphemy against the Spirit can be worse than blasphemy against the Son only if the Spirit is also divine.

IV.   THE HOLY SPIRIT IS CALLED GOD

Finally, we believe the Holy Spirit is divine because the Bible specifically speaks of Him as God. When the Apostle Peter addresses Ananias' deceit in Acts 5:1-4, he asks him, "Why has Satan filled your heart to lie to the Holy Spirit … ?" He then characterizes this lie thus: "You have not lied to men but to God." Thus Peter specifically equates the Holy Spirit with God; lying to the Spirit is the same as lying to God.

Another such text is 1 Corinthians 3:16, "Do you not know that you are a temple of God and that the Spirit of God dwells in you?" Using the analogy or type of the Old Testament temple as the literal locale of the Shekinah glory, the visible manifestation of God to the Jews (Exodus 40:34-38), Paul says the church is God's temple, God's dwelling-place today; and we are indwelt specifically by "the Spirit of God." See also Ephesians 2:22, "You also are being built together into a dwelling of God in the Spirit." The same applies to the body of the individual believer (1 Corinthians 6:19).

The Bible identifies the Holy Spirit as God in a very dramatic way when Old Testament events and sayings of which Yahweh (the LORD) is the subject are in the New Testament attributed to the Holy Spirit. One such New Testament text is Acts 28:25-27, where Paul directly cites Isaiah 6:8-10. Whereas Paul says, "the Holy Spirit rightly spoke through Isaiah the prophet," the Old Testament text clearly places the quoted words in the mouth of Yahweh (the LORD). The same is true of Hebrews 10:15-17 and Jeremiah 31:31-34. Hebrews says that in these words "the Holy Spirit also testifies to us," while Jeremiah clearly shows that they are the declaration of Yahweh (the LORD). Based on these texts, Rene Pache says, "The Spirit is therefore undeniably God Himself" (*The Person and*

Work of the Holy Spirit [Marshall, Morgan & Scott, 1956], 16-17). John F. Walvoord agrees: "The title of Jehovah, reserved in Scripture for the true God, is therefore used of the Holy Spirit" (*The Holy Spirit* [Zondervan, 1991], 12).

THE HOLY SPIRIT IN THE LIFE OF JESUS

Our Trinitarian God includes the three divine persons of the Father, the Son, and the Holy Spirit, all of whom are equal in their existence, their nature, and their authority. When we make such statements as this, we are speaking of what is called the *ontological* Trinity, where the emphasis is on their unity and equality. We also speak of the *economic* Trinity, where the various different works of the three persons are distinguished.

Regarding the economic Trinity, the one element in the catalogue of Trinitarian activities that stretches our minds the most is the incarnation of God the Son in the human person, Jesus of Nazareth. From the standpoint of God's purposes, nature, and wisdom, the incarnation was required as the only way that sinners might be redeemed from the punishment due to their sins. We recognize that this event of the incarnation was absolutely radical and drastic, and we marvel that God was willing to go to this extreme to save us.

Simply trying to understand all that was involved in God the Son's union with the man Jesus is a tremendous challenge. Since Jesus was a combination of two natures (divine and human) in one person (one center of consciousness), it is extremely difficult to sort out which nature was "in the driver's seat" at various points along the way in Jesus's ministry. The temptation is to assume that anything requiring supernatural powers would just naturally come from His divine nature. But this raises the question of how Jesus and the Holy Spirit were connected during the Savior's earthly ministry. We know that there was a connection, but how and why?

This essay addresses these questions. We probably will not be able to answer them as fully as we would like, given that the Trinity and the incarnation are the two most mysterious of all theological issues. I have found, though, that concerning the connection between the earthly Jesus and the Holy Spirit, there is a lot more about this in the Gospels than we usually notice. And some of what we find there may be a bit surprising to us, as we now begin to explore it. (For more on the subject, see chapter 4, "The Holy Spirit and Jesus Christ," in my book, *Power from on High: What the Bible Says About the Holy Spirit* [College Press, 2007], pp. 127-153. Scripture quotations in this essay are from the NASB unless noted.)

I.   THE FACT: JESUS WAS FILLED WITH THE HOLY SPIRIT

The Old Testament prophesies that the coming Messiah would be empowered by the "Spirit of the Lord." This is affirmed three times in the book of Isaiah. First, Isaiah 11:1-2 says, "Then a shoot will spring from the stem of Jesse, and a branch from his roots will bear fruit. The Spirit of the LORD will rest on Him, the spirit of wisdom and understanding, the spirit of counsel and strength, the spirit of knowledge and the fear of the LORD." This text is not cited in the New Testament. One that is cited is Isaiah 42:1, "Behold, My Servant, whom I uphold; My chosen one *in whom* My soul delights. I have put My Spirit upon Him; He will bring forth justice to the nations." This is quoted in Matthew 12:17.

Another such text is Isaiah 61:1-2, cited in the narrative of Luke 4:17-21. In Isaiah the text reads, "The Spirit of the Lord GOD is upon me, because the LORD has anointed me to bring good news to the afflicted; He has sent me to bind up the brokenhearted, to proclaim liberty to captives and freedom to prisoners; to proclaim the favorable year of the LORD and the day of vengeance of our God; to comfort all who mourn." Jesus Himself quotes this in a Sabbath service; Luke records the recitation thus: "The Spirit of the Lord is upon Me, because He anointed Me to preach the gospel to the poor. He has sent Me to proclaim release to the captives, and recovery of sight to the blind, to set free those who are oppressed, to proclaim the favorable year of the Lord." Then Luke reports how Jesus declared that He was the fulfillment of this prophecy: "Today this Scripture has been fulfilled in your hearing" (v. 21).

In other places the Gospels report that Jesus was filled with the Spirit. Just after His baptism and just prior to His forty days of temptation, Luke 4:1 says, "Jesus, full of the Holy Spirit, returned from the Jordan and was led around by the Spirit in the wilderness for forty days." Afterwards, "Jesus returned to Galilee in the power of the Spirit" (Luke 4:14).

John 3:34 gives us this comment: "For He whom God has sent speaks the words of God; for He gives the Spirit without measure." The NIV translates the last part thus: "For God gives the Spirit without limit." The record here does not specify that *Jesus* was the one to whom the Spirit was given, but the context gives ample support for this interpretation. The KJV thus translates it, "For God giveth not the Spirit by measure *unto him*" (the italics meaning that these words are not in the original text). In his *Gospel According to John* (Eerdmans 1971, pp. 246-247), Leon Morris says that this is the "preferable" meaning.

This of course raises the question, if Jesus Himself was *divine*, why did he *need* to be filled with the Spirit? Jesus was indeed fully divine, and He was also fully human. At least from the beginning of His ministry, His life was filled with supernatural deeds. Shall we simply assume that this was His divine nature at work? I admit that this was my own assumption before I made this present study. As an analogy, I imagined a motorcycle with a sidecar, and thus with a driver and a passenger. I was picturing

Christ's divine nature sitting in the driver's seat, with his human nature in the sidecar.

But now I do not think it is necessarily that way. Although Jesus was indeed fully divine, we know from Philippians 2:7 that the Logos, God the Son, voluntarily suspended the use of at least some of His divine powers when He became a human being. We know that His omniscience was somehow affected (Matthew 24:36). Such suspensions were made in order to allow Jesus's human nature to be fully operative during His ministry years.

Thus it seems to be that Jesus was performing supernatural deeds *as a human being* who was completely filled with the Holy Spirit. We should remember the Spirit-empowered prophets and miracle-workers in the Old Testament era. Most (but not all) of the things Jesus did (involving miracles and revelation) were not qualitatively different from the things Moses, Elijah, Isaiah, and even John the Baptist had already done, as a result of *their* being filled with the Holy Spirit. In a way very similar to these humble servants, the Spirit-enabled human nature of Jesus was fully involved in His mighty works throughout His ministry.

II.   THE TIME WHEN JESUS WAS FILLED WITH THE SPIRIT

We cannot deny the *fact* that Jesus was filled with the Holy Spirit, but this fact raises another question, namely, *when* did this filling occur? Two main possibilities have been suggested: at His birth, or at His baptism.

Some say Jesus was filled with the Spirit at His birth (or even earlier, at His conception). We know that the Holy Spirit was the divine agent who supernaturally caused the human person, Jesus, to begin to grow in Mary's womb. Luke 1:35 says, "The angel answered and said to her, 'The Holy Spirit will come upon you, and the power of the Most High will overshadow you; and for that reason the holy Child shall be called the Son of God." Matthew 1:18 says of Joseph and Mary, "Before they came together she was found to be with child by the Holy Spirit." An angel confirmed this to Joseph in a dream: "The Child who has been conceived in her is of the Holy Spirit" (v. 20).

Exactly what was the Holy Spirit doing at the moment of the supernatural conception of Jesus in Mary's womb? We may distinguish two—and possibly three—distinct divine acts. First was the miraculous transformation of a naturally-produced ovum in Mary's womb into the fully human male person, Jesus. This happened without the addition of the chromosomes usually provided by a male sperm. This was the specific work of the Holy Spirit as the divine agent, in the moment when He "came upon" and "overshadowed" Mary. This work of the Spirit was not performed on Mary's body, but upon the ovum.

The second divine act was the joining of the eternal, personal, divine Logos, the second person of the Trinity, with this newly-formed human being. "The Word became flesh" (John 1:14). This was not the Spirit's work, but that of the Logos. We do not and cannot understand the details of this.

The possible third divine act that may have occurred at this time was that the infant Jesus was (possibly) prevented, by divine intervention, from receiving any negative effects from Adam's sin. This is a common idea, and is often given as the rationale for the "virgin birth" of Jesus. All we can say here is that it was *possible* that divine intervention was necessary to preserve Jesus's human nature from the effects of Adam's sin (i.e., from "original sin"), and it was *possible* that this was the Holy Spirit's work. However, this is actually just speculation; and, even if it was so, this would have nothing to do with the virgin birth of Jesus.

The fact is, though, that none of these two and possibly three divine interventions associated with Christ's birth are related to His being filled with the Holy Spirit. If the filling occurred at his birth (or conception), it would have been a distinct and separate act. And some say this is exactly what happened, in a way similar to what happened with John the Baptist, of whom it was said: "He will be filled with the Holy Spirit while yet in his mother's womb" (Luke 1:15). Some affirm this was true also of Jesus: "What was said of John the Baptist surely could be said of our Lord, that He was filled with the Holy Spirit from His birth," says Don DeWelt (*The Power of the Holy Spirit* [College Press, 1971], III:9). John Walvoord says it is a "reasonable inference" that Jesus was so filled from His conception (*The Holy Spirit* [Zondervan, 1991], p. 92). This was never specifically said, however.

If the man Jesus were indeed filled with the Holy Spirit at or near the beginning of His existence, what would be the purpose? Two possibilities have been suggested. Some say this was to impart *ministerial power* or service gifts to Jesus, i.e., equipping Him with miraculous and non-miraculous spiritual gifts. Others say it was to impart *moral power* to Jesus, i.e., the ability to resist all sin and live a perfect life.

Those who affirm the latter attribute Jesus's perfect holiness and sinlessness to the Spirit's presence within Him. Edwin Palmer compares Jesus's being filled with the Spirit, with the way the Holy Spirit indwells Christians; thus the Spirit "was the author of the holiness in Jesus' human nature" (*The Person and Ministry of the Holy Spirit* [Baker, 1974], p. 67). He continues, "All the time, ... even as a baby, he was indwelt by the Spirit." All of His spiritual growth "was due to the operation of the Holy Spirit" in His life" (pp. 68-69). Abraham Kuyper asserts that human nature without the Holy Spirit cannot produce holiness, not even in Jesus (*The Work of the Holy Spirit* [Eerdmans, 1966], p. 102-103, 110).

I reject this idea totally. The Spirit's indwelling as a source of power for resisting sin and producing holiness is the gift given from the Day of Pentecost and following (see Acts 2), as the new blessing of the Holy Spirit promised for the Messianic age. It was not given to any Old Testament saints, and is never identified as a necessary prerequisite for sinlessness as such. It is pure speculation to suggest that this is why Jesus received the Holy Spirit at all.

Others say that Jesus's alleged natal or prenatal filling with the Spirit endowed Him with "every spiritual gift from the moment of conception" (Walvoord, p. 93). I agree that this was the *purpose* for Jesus's being filled with the Spirit, but I see no reason to believe that it happened at or before His birth. A better case can be made for the following.

The other main view of the *time* when Jesus was filled with the Holy Spirit says that He was filled at His *baptism*. It is important to remember that Jesus's baptism, though received in the context of John the Baptist's ministry to all Israelites, was totally unique. As far as its meaning is concerned, it has no parallel with Christian baptism, and little similarity with John's baptism as received by others. It was part of Jesus's inauguration for His unique ministry. And the unique thing that most stands out about His baptism is the way it was connected with the Holy Spirit.

All four gospels report the descent of the dove upon Jesus immediately after He was baptized (see Matthew 3:16; Mark 1:10; Luke 3:21-22; John 1:32-33). This was a literal dove, most likely created *ex nihilo* for this theophany of the Holy Spirit. John the Baptist and (probably) Jesus Himself saw the dove, but did not see the invisible Spirit Himself. Nevertheless all four Gospels are very clear that this was not *just* a dove, but was the *Holy Spirit* in the form of a dove, descending and "lighting upon" Jesus (Matthew 3:16), and "remaining" upon Him (John 1:33). John the Baptist reported that God Himself referred to the Spirit—not just the dove—as "descending and remaining upon" Jesus.

It is significant that the statement in Luke 4:1—that Jesus was "full of the Holy Spirit"—follows directly after the baptism of Jesus (as far as the historical record is concerned). This supports the view that the filling with the Holy Spirit was at Jesus's baptism, not His birth.

This then leads to the further conclusion that the filling with the Spirit, as connected with the baptism itself, was to anoint and empower Jesus for his imminent ministry as prophet, priest, and king. This was Jesus' *inauguration* for His ministry, and the Spirit was given to Him specifically as an empowerment for His work.

This would be parallel to the anointing of David as king (1 Samuel 16:13), the anointing of Elisha as prophet (1 Kings 19:16), and the anointing of priests (Exodus 29:7; Leviticus 8:10-13, 30). These are *ordination* services. The use of oil symbolized the outpouring of the Holy Spirit on these men, as 1 Samuel 16:13 says of David: "Then Samuel took the horn of oil and anointed him in the midst of his brothers; and the Spirit of the LORD came mightily upon David from that day forward." For Jesus, the supernatural appearance of the dove takes the place of the oil. "God anointed Him with the Holy Spirit and with power" (Acts 10:38). Jesus thus is truly *the Christ*, the "anointed one." As Isaiah 61:1 says, "The Spirit of the Lord God is upon me, because the LORD has **anointed** me" (see Luke 4:18). See also Isaiah 42:1, as cited in Matthew 12:18.

III. THE PURPOSE FOR JESUS'S FILLING WITH THE SPIRIT

We have already indicated that Jesus's filling with the Spirit was to empower Him for the work of His mission as the Christ. Here we want to emphasize that He was filled with the Spirit "without limit" (John 3:34, NIV), so that now, AS A MAN—as a HUMAN BEING—He may be fully equipped with supernatural power, thus enabling Him to accomplish His Messianic tasks *as a human being*. He enters upon His public ministry "in the power of the Spirit" (Luke 4:14).

Jesus the man is now equipped to fulfill His *prophetic* ministry. A prophet of God is someone who speaks inspired messages from God. Such inspiration is the work of the Holy Spirit. Now, Jesus was God's prophet *par excellence*: Deuteronomy 18:17-18; Acts 3:22; 7:37. Every word Jesus spoke was a word from God, not just because He Himself *was* divine, but also because He was filled with the Spirit. See the relation between Jesus's anointing with the Spirit and His ministry of preaching and proclamation: Luke 4:17-19 (Isaiah 61:1-2).

Also, Jesus the man is now equipped to fulfill His *kingly* ministry. This begins with Jesus's decisive encounter with and defeat of the devil, also known as the *temptation* of Jesus, which followed immediately after the Spirit came upon Him in His baptism (Matthew 4:1-11; Mark 1:12-13; Luke 4:1-13). This was not just a coincidence. Jesus was "led up by the Spirit" to this encounter, says Matthew (v. 1). Indeed, "Immediately the Spirit impelled Him to go out into the wilderness," says Mark 1:12. The word "impelled" is *ekballō*, which is a very strong Greek word. It implies that the Holy Spirit was not passive in this encounter, but took the initiative.

Once in the wilderness Jesus "was led around by the Spirit ... for forty days, being tempted by the devil" (Luke 4:1-2). "Being tempted" is a present participle, suggesting that the encounter with the devil occupied the entire forty days. The three recorded temptations are simply typical. Mark 1:13 says, "He was in the wilderness forty days being tempted by Satan." And the Holy Spirit was with Him *the entire time*, to empower Him—for what?

Some say the Spirit's role was simply to give Jesus the man enough moral power to resist the devil's temptations (as He does for us through His indwelling presence), and thus to remain sinless. I have already expressed my objection to the idea that Jesus needed the Holy Spirit in order to remain sinless. His being "filled with the Spirit" was NOT equivalent to the post-Pentecostal gift of the indwelling of the Spirit as our source of moral power. The terminology of being "filled with the Spirit" is used for empowerment for service, too (cf., e.g., Exodus 31:1-3).

And what was going on with Jesus during these forty days was not *merely* temptation. It was not just a moral struggle to maintain his sinlessness.

Looking at the encounter with Satan merely in this way seriously underestimates the significance of this forty-day period. This was not just a time of temptation, but was Jesus's initial confrontation with "the god of this world" (2 Corinthians 4:4). Jesus is beginning the process of *destroying the works of the devil* (1 John 3:8), of ousting the devil from his usurped role as "the ruler of this world" (John 12:31), and of establishing His own *kingship* over all things.

Satan did not initiate this confrontation; GOD did, when the Spirit *impelled* Jesus into the wilderness. As God's champion He is "calling out" the devil, or throwing down the gauntlet, so to speak. As the second Adam He is beginning His work of crushing the serpent's head (Genesis 3:15) and reversing the Edenic curse. He is beginning His work of binding the devil (Matthew 12:29; Revelation 20:1-3) and rendering him powerless (Hebrews 2:14). As the Messianic King He is confronting His enemies (Psalms 2, 45) and setting up His kingdom (Matthew 12:28).

And in this forty-day period Jesus is doing all of this *as a human being*! No wonder He needed the empowerment of the Holy Spirit! His battle against the devil in the wilderness was on a completely different level from the ordinary temptations faced by ordinary people. We must not equate our own spiritual warfare with what was happening during those forty days. At His baptism Jesus was anointed with the Holy Spirit and with power (Acts 10:38) for the very purpose of encountering and defeating the devil *on a cosmic scale*.

Jesus's subsequent encounters with and dominance over demons were a major aspect of His kingly ministry, for which He was empowered by the Spirit: "But if I cast out demons **by the Spirit of God**, then the kingdom of God has come upon you" (Matthew 12:28; see Luke 4:18). It may be that Jesus the man worked all of His miracles through the power with which the Spirit filled Him. Without doubt His bodily resurrection

was (at least in part) the work of the Holy Spirit (Romans 1:4; 8:11; 1
Peter 3:18).

Finally, we will note that Jesus the man, once filled with the Spirit in
His baptism, was equipped to fulfill His *priestly* ministry. Jesus's priestly
work was the offering of Himself as the sacrifice for our sins, and we are
told that He "**through the eternal Spirit** offered Himself without blemish
to God" (Hebrews 9:14). In my judgment this means that the Holy Spirit
was the source of the strength which enabled Jesus's *human* nature to
undergo the ordeal by which His divine nature was bearing the wrath of
God for the sins of the world, probably beginning in Gethsemane.

It is in His priestly work that the *divine* nature of Jesus becomes most
essential, since only Jesus as the *divine* Son of God can, in a finite span of
time, literally suffer the eternal consequences of sin for any one human
being, much less for the whole human race. *Possibly*, all His priestly work
up to this point *could* have been accomplished by Jesus as a human being,
empowered by the Spirit. But here in His substitutionary atonement,
Christ's divine nature is especially operative and engaged. But still, the
divine nature of Jesus cannot go through this priestly process without the
human nature as well. Jesus cannot just "turn off" His human nature
here—but how will He as a human being be *able* to endure what now lies
before Him?

In the few hours Jesus spent in the garden of grief (Matthew 26:38),
every strand of His Messianic purpose came together and was unfolded
before His human nature as never before. When He became aware of the
magnitude, the enormity, the infinite weight of the burden He was about
to bear, His first reaction was to recoil: "My Father, if it is possible, let this
cup pass from Me" (Matthew 26:39).

The cosmic scale of the task that lay immediately before Him at this
point was comparable to what took place during the forty days of
"temptation." Then, of course, He was confronting the devil as an enemy
who was using every means at His disposal to prevent the Messiah from

accomplishing His purpose. Then, the Spirit gave Him the strength necessary to resist Satan's adversarial power. Here in Gethsemane, there is no indication of the tempter's presence. The dialogue is between Jesus and His heavenly Father, and both are on the same side; both are of the same purpose. Jesus's hesitation comes not from a moral weakness being exploited by Satan, but from the simple finitude of His human nature. He is overwhelmed by the seeming impossibility of this next step in His Messianic journey.

As He continues to pray, though, His initial recoiling disappears, and His mind and heart are calmed and made ready for the unspeakable ordeal that awaits Him: "My Father, if this cannot pass away unless I drink it, Your will be done" (Matthew 26:42).   If there was a specific point when "the eternal Spirit" strengthened the man Jesus Christ in the shadow of Calvary, this was it. Here we can picture the power of the Spirit undergirding the finite humanity of Jesus and infusing Him with the resolve to see His "mission impossible" through to the end.

This is of course an inference, but it seems sound. If the Spirit's presence empowered Jesus throughout His earthly ministry, which it did, surely there was no point in this ministry where the Spirit's power was more needed than here.

CONCLUSION

For Jesus to accomplish His Messianic purposes, He had to be both fully divine and fully human. But what He had to accomplish in His divine nature, especially in reference to the atonement, required more than finite human nature by its own resources can achieve. To enable His human nature to "keep up with" His divine nature, so to speak, Jesus was given the supernatural power of the Holy Spirit.

JESUS AND THE POWER OF THE HOLY SPIRIT

QUESTION: Is the following statement true? I.e., "Jesus's strength does not come from His individual power, but from His relationship with the other persons of the Trinity." I am hesitant to say this because I want to exalt Christ, and yet the Bible speaks of Him going about in the power of the Spirit.

ANSWER: The statement is basically true, but I would say it like this: "Jesus's strength comes NOT ONLY from His own power, BUT ALSO from His relationship with the other persons of the Trinity." I have discussed this whole issue in great detail in my book on the Holy Spirit, *Power from on High: What the Bible Says About the Holy Spirit* (College Press, 2007), in ch. 4, "The Holy Spirit and Jesus Christ," pp. 127-153. I have also summarized that material in an earlier essay in this book. Nevertheless, I have decided to respond to the question above by presenting here my conclusion to chapter 4 in the book which I have just mentioned, pp. 152-153.

Whatever were the relationships among the persons of the Trinity prior to creation, prior to the incarnation, and prior to Pentecost, in their works in relation to the world and especially in relation to redemption these divine persons have taken upon themselves relationships that did not necessarily exist in their eternally preexistent state. One type of relationship that the persons of the Trinity assumed in their creative and redemptive purposes was a relationship of authority and submission. Since this kind of relationship was assumed (voluntarily entered into) by the Trinitarian persons, it implies no inequality in their essence, authority, and power.

The incarnation itself is a major example of how these assumed relationships of authority and submission take shape in the course of God's working out of the redemptive plan. In the incarnation the eternal, divine Logos became a human person, Jesus of Nazareth. The result was that this unique person has two natures: a fully divine nature, and a fully human nature.

In his divine nature, Jesus is fully God, with all the attributes of God in place. In the incarnation He did not lose or surrender any of His divine essence or attributes. But this raises a serious question: if Jesus was fully divine, why did He need to be filled with the Spirit? The answer is, because He was also fully human, and for the purposes of His redemptive mission His human nature had to be fully operative. For this to be the case, in His divine-human personhood as Jesus of Nazareth, God the eternal Logos voluntarily placed Himself in the role of a servant to God the Father. As Jesus of Nazareth He submits himself to the Father's will and authority. (See Cottrell, *The Faith Once for All* [College Press, 2002], pp. 255-257.)

Also, in order to allow His human nature to be fully operative, in His incarnation Jesus voluntarily surrendered or suspended the use of at least some of His divine attributes. (This is the point of Philippians 2:6-7.) He came to earth as a man; He was born, He grew up, and He lived among men as a man. But what He had to accomplish as the Messiah required more than human nature by its own resources can achieve. However, rather than using His own divine nature for His tasks, He used the supernatural power of the Holy Spirit. Explaining how this was so is what this chapter has been about. We have seen, as H. Leo Boles says, that Christ assumed a "dependence upon the Holy Spirit" (*The Holy Spirit*

[Gospel Advocate, 1956], p. 128), not necessarily for His holy living, but for His supernatural works. As Bruce Ware says, "Although Jesus was fully God, as a man he chose to rely not on his own divine nature but on the power of the Spirit" (*Father, Son, and Holy Spirit* [Crossway, 2005] p. 91).

How was His dependence on the Spirit different from Old Testament prophets, priests, and kings? The difference is not qualitative, but quantitative. This is the point of John 3:34. The uniqueness of Christ's mission required that the Father give Him the Spirit without measure, to empower and equip Him for this mission. If this is indeed the main way the Spirit worked in the life of Jesus, and I believe it is, we must not try to draw too many parallels between the Spirit in Jesus's life and the Spirit in our own lives as Christians.

(As an added note, it is commendable to want to exalt Christ in every appropriate way, but it is unbiblical to exalt Christ in all possible ways. A major example is the desire to make Christ—His example, His work of redemption, His teachings in the gospels—the ultimate norm for all ethics and all theological truth. I call this the "Christological fallacy," i.e., the error of exalting Christ in the area of epistemology when we should be focusing on his primary work of redemption. I discuss that a bit in my book on God the Creator, in a section called "The Primacy of Creation," pp. 171ff.)

THE HOLY SPIRIT AND THE
FIRST-CENTURY CHURCH

The Holy Spirit, as one of the three persons of the Trinity, has been working alongside the Father and the Son since the world began (Genesis 1:2). He was involved in the life of God's people, Israel, from the days of Moses onward (Numbers 11:17, 25; Isaiah 63:10-12). When the Church took the place of Israel as the people of God, the Spirit continued His work and indeed added a new blessing, as indicated in the second chapter of Acts. He will continue to work among God's people throughout this age and in the age everlasting.

This present essay focuses upon the Holy Spirit's activity within the first-century church. I will explain especially how His work from the Day of Pentecost (Acts 2) onward was in continuity with His work in the Old Testament era, and I will give special emphasis to the new work that began on that day. I will present the Spirit's work in terms of the kinds of *gifts* that he bestows upon the Lord's people. These gifts may be understood as various kinds of *abilities* he bestows upon us. We may distinguish four kinds of such abilities or gifts.

I.   TRUTH GIFTS

We know that God has created human beings in His own image, partly for the very purpose of enabling us to communicate with Him, i.e., to relate to Him through the means of human language. In Bible days God at times spoke directly to chosen individuals and groups; such communication would naturally be received as absolutely truthful and authoritative. In most cases, though, God chose to use human instruments as an indirect means of communicating His truth to others. These chosen ones functioned as prophets, speaking messages from God that were supernaturally *given*, through revelation; and if not supernaturally given, at least supernaturally *approved*, through inspiration.

The Holy Spirit was directly involved in the minds and bodies of those chosen to receive and communicate truth from God to others. The Spirit gave them the ability to speak or write this truth as the very Word of God and without error (2 Peter 1:19-21). In Old Testament times God spoke thus through His prophets (cf. 2 Samuel 23:2; Acts 1:16; 1 Peter 1:10-12). In the first-century church some were chosen to receive the Spirit's gift of prophecy (1 Corinthians 12:10, 28; Ephesians 4:11), but the main ones who received these truth gifts were the apostles.

Jesus gave the apostles His special promise to send them the Holy Spirit for the very purpose of enabling them to speak the truth that He Himself wanted to communicate to His people through them (John 14:26; 15:26; 16:12-14; Acts 1:8). The first exercise of this truth gift was Peter's sermon on Pentecost, Acts 2:14-40. The apostles (and New Testament prophets, Ephesians 2:20; 3:5) continued to speak and write God's inerrant Word throughout their lives in the first-century church.

Many of us, including myself, believe that the truth gifts from the Spirit ceased after the apostolic age, since the need for new truth ceased once God's new redemptive work through Christ had been fully explained (1 Corinthians 13:8-13).

II.   SIGN GIFTS

The second type of gift bestowed on selected individuals is the ability to work miracles. A miracle is an event that is contrary to the laws of nature, in the sense that it cannot be the result of natural causes. God can perform miraculous deeds directly (e.g., the burning bush, Exodus 3:2; the resurrection of Jesus), but He can also empower human individuals to invoke miraculous powers and perform miracles. Such miraculous powers are a gift of the Holy Spirit (1 Corinthians 12:9-10). We call them "sign gifts" because the purpose of miracles is to be a sign (confirmation, evidence, proof) of the truth given through the truth gifts explained above.

The Spirit was giving such powers in Old Testament times; we know especially of Moses and Elijah as miracle-workers. The apostles were given these gifts even before Pentecost (Matthew 10:1); and they continued to exercise them in the first-century church (Acts 2:43; 5:12; 2 Corinthians 12:12), as did many others upon whom the apostles laid their hands (Acts 6:6, 8; Acts 8:14-19; Acts 19:6).

It is extremely important to understand that such sign gifts, like the truth gifts above, were not something new that began on the Day of Pentecost. This is especially important for understanding the gift of speaking in tongues, both on Pentecost and at other times in the early church. The miraculous ability to speak in unlearned languages or to speak in a miraculous manner was not a new thing and was not the main point of Pentecost. The Holy Spirit had already given this ability at least once in Old Testament times (Numbers 11:24-30). The main purpose of this miraculous speaking, both in Numbers 11 and in Acts 2, was to be a sign of the truth of the revelation it accompanied. In Numbers 11 it confirmed God's promise that the Holy Spirit was now present on the 70 assistants of Moses; in Acts 2 the gift of speaking in tongues was for the *sole purpose* of proving the truth of Peter's Pentecost sermon beginning in v. 14. There was nothing new about it.

Many of us, including myself, believe that the sign gifts, like the truth gifts, ceased after the apostolic age, since miraculous signs would no longer be needed when the revelation of new truth ceased (1 Corinthians 13:8-13).

III.   SERVICE GIFTS

The third kind of gift bestowed by the Spirit can be called "service gifts," since their purpose was to empower individuals to perform ordinary (not miraculous) tasks to serve the ongoing needs of the people of God. The Spirit was giving such gifts in Old Testament times, e.g., the ability to do the work of craftsmen for the building of the tabernacle (Exodus 31:1-5; 35:30-35; 36:1-2), and the ability to serve as leaders (e.g., Numbers 11:17; Deuteronomy 34:9; Judges 6:34; 1 Samuel 16:13).

Most of the "spiritual gifts' mentioned in the New Testament lists of such gifts are of this nature; see Romans 12:8, Ephesians 4:11, and 1 Corinthians 12. These were nothing new, and they continue to be given to God's people today according to the needs of the body of Christ as a whole.

IV.   SALVATION GIFTS

The most important way the Holy Spirit worked in the first-century church is to provide *salvation* gifts to everyone who accepted Jesus Christ as Lord and Savior. This was the new work of the Spirit that began on the Day of Pentecost. Whatever the reason, God was not bestowing these gifts upon Old Testament saints; they are part of the continuing blessings of the Messianic age. These gifts were first given in Acts 2, and they have been given to new converts ever since.

Though begun at Pentecost, this saving work of the Spirit was promised long before. Isaiah 43:19-20 promises a new thing which is explained in Isaiah 44:3, "For I will pour water on the thirsty land, and streams on the dry ground; I will pour my Spirit upon your offspring" (ESV). See also Ezekiel 36:25-27 and Joel 2:28-32 (the latter is quoted by Peter in Acts 2:16ff.). John the Baptist promised that Jesus would baptize with the Holy Spirit and with fire (Matthew 3:11; Mark 1:8; Luke 3:16; John 1:32-33). This promise does NOT refer to miraculous gifts, especially the gift of tongues; it refers to the new salvation gifts of which Peter speaks in Acts 2:38-39 (see 1 Corinthians 12:13). Jesus promises the same thing in Luke 11:13; John 4:10, 13-14; 7:37-39; Acts 1:4-5.

Exactly what is this new work of the Spirit, this new gift of the Spirit, begun on Pentecost? The main gift, of course, is the Holy Spirit Himself, promised by the Father and poured out with accompanying miraculous signs into the midst of the apostles (Acts 2:1-4, 33). From that point on this promised Divine Presence has been ready to enter into the hearts and bodies on anyone who will obey the gospel as Peter presented it in Acts 2:38-39, "Repent and be baptized every one of you in the name of Jesus Christ for the forgiveness of your sins, and you will receive the gift of the Holy Spirit. For the promise is for you [the immediate Jewish audience] and for your children [your descendants from now on] and for all who are far off [the Gentiles, too!]."

Once we have obeyed the gospel and have received the indwelling presence of the Spirit (Romans 8:9-11; 1 Corinthians 6:19-20), the Spirit immediately begins to bestow upon us the salvation gifts which are His main work in this New Covenant age. These are the immediate gift of regeneration, Titus 3:5 (the new birth, John 3:5; the new creation, 2 Corinthians 5:17; resurrection from spiritual death, Colossians 2:12); and the ongoing gift of sanctification. Through the gift of sanctification the indwelling Spirit empowers us to be holy as God is holy (1 Peter 1:15-16), to put sin to death in our lives (Romans 8:13), to resist temptation (1 Corinthians 10:13), and to produce the fruit of the Spirit (Galatians 5:22-24). See Ephesians 3:16; Philippians 2:12-13; 1 John 4:4.

These salvation gifts of the Spirit are the essence of the Spirit's ongoing work in the Church. They were the climax of Pentecost and are the treasure of the Church today. May we not eclipse them by overemphasizing the Spirit's other gifts, however important they have been and may continue to be today.

Note: this item first appeared in the July 17/24, 2011, issue of the *Christian Standard*. It is included here with the kind permission of Christian Standard Media.

ARE MIRACULOUS GIFTS THE BLESSING OF PENTECOST?

This essay originally appeared in the *Christian Standard*, May 9, 1982, pp. 9-11. It was then presented at a breakout (workshop) session at the July 30, 1982, North American Christian Convention theological forum in Kansas City, MO, under the title, "The Gift and the Gifts of the Holy Spirit." It is printed here with the permission of Christian Standard Media.

INTRODUCTION

Pentecost! We all know what happened on the Day of Pentecost in Acts 2, as far as the Holy Spirit is concerned. The Pentecostals know what happened. The "Charismatics" know what happened. Alexander Campbell knew what happened, and so did J. W. McGarvey. Likewise, all of us in the Restoration Movement today know what happened on Pentecost.

Or do we?

Sure we do. We all know that on Pentecost the Holy Spirit empowered a few people to do something *miraculous*—i.e., speaking in tongues! This is it. This is the blessing of Pentecost.

Or is it?

I am speaking specifically of the Holy Spirit's relation to the day of Pentecost. My purpose here is to call for a re-examination of the essence of Pentecost. I believe that Pentecostals and Restoration Movement traditionalists alike have missed the point of the Pentecostal blessing by equating it with miraculous powers.

This has had two tragic effects. First, it has led many believers to expect miraculous gifts to be available to all Christians in all ages. Second, it has drawn attention away from the *real* new blessing of the New Testament age, i.e., the indwelling presence of the Spirit as the source of *moral* (not miraculous) power.

The gist of what follows can be summed up like this: The Pentecostal blessing was promised to be something new; miraculous gifts were nothing new; therefore miraculous gifts were not the blessing of Pentecost.

I.   THE PROMISE

To see this more clearly we must first note the prominent stream of prophecies and promises of the Spirit's coming. This promise is not obscure and incidental; it is actually a major prophetic theme which creates a strong expectation leading up to Pentecost.

Isaiah 43:19-21 reveals God's plan to do a new thing, something that would involve the outpouring of life-giving water: "Behold, I will do something new, now it will spring forth; will you not be aware of it? I will even make a roadway in the wilderness, rivers in the desert. The beasts of the field will glorify Me, the jackals and the ostriches, because I have given waters in the wilderness and rivers in the desert, to give drink to My chosen people. The people whom I formed for Myself will declare My praise." Isaiah 44:3-4 then explains this promise further: "For I will pour out water on the thirsty *land* and streams on the dry ground; I will pour out My Spirit on your offspring and My blessing on your descendants; and they will spring up among the grass like poplars by streams of water."

Ezekiel 36:25-27 should also be noted: "Then I will sprinkle clean water on you, and you will be clean; I will cleanse you from all your filthiness and from all your idols. Moreover, I will give you a new heart and put a new spirit within you; and I will remove the heart of stone from your flesh and give you a heart of flesh. I will put My Spirit within you and cause you to walk in My statutes, and you will be careful to observe My ordinances."

Then of course comes the great prophecy in Joel 2:28-29: "It will come about after this that I will pour out My Spirit on all mankind; and your sons and daughters will prophesy, your old men will dream dreams, your young men will see visions. Even on the male and female servants I will pour out My Spirit in those days."

This prophetic theme is continued in the New Testament. John the Baptist stated it thus in Matthew 3:11: "As for me, I baptize you with water for repentance, but He who is coming after me is mightier than I, and I am not fit to remove His sandals; He will baptize you with the Holy Spirit and fire." (See also Mark 1:7-8; Luke 3:16; John 1:33.)

In Luke 11:13 Jesus said, "If you then, being evil, know how to give good gifts to your children, how much more will *your* heavenly Father give the Holy Spirit to those who ask Him?" Jesus restated the promise more specifically in John 7:37-39: "Now on the last day, the great *day* of the feast, Jesus stood and cried out, saying, 'If anyone is thirsty, let him come to Me and drink. He who believes in Me, as the Scripture said, "From his innermost being will flow rivers of living water."' But this He spoke of the Spirit, whom those who believed in Him were to receive; for the Spirit was not yet *given*, because Jesus was not yet glorified."

In His private conference with His apostles on crucifixion eve, Jesus disclosed that the coming of the Spirit would have special meaning and results for them in view of their unique relation to Him and their authoritative role in the church. See John 14:16-17, 26; 15:26-27; 16:7-15. We must remember that these promises were given in a private conversation between Jesus and His apostles. These are promises concerning revelation and inspiration, and were directed here to the

Apostles alone. These are not part of the stream of prophecies and promises given to the people of God in general.

After His resurrection and before His ascension, Jesus renewed all these promises of the outpouring of the Holy Spirit. Luke 24:49 gives this summary of the words of Jesus as He spoke them to His apostles: "And behold, I am sending forth the promise of My Father upon you, but you are to stay in the city until you are clothed with power from on high." The first chapter of the Book of Acts records the distinct promises of the Holy Spirit in a bit more detail. In Acts 1:4-5 Jesus tells the apostles not to leave Jerusalem but to wait for what the Father had promised, which "you heard of from Me; for John baptized with water, but you will be baptized with the Holy Spirit not many days from now." This seems to be referring to the general promise that had begun with Isaiah 43:19-21. But then, just before the ascension, Jesus refers back to the promises He had made specifically to the apostles in John 14-16: "But you will receive power when the Holy Spirit has come upon you; and you shall be My witnesses both in Jerusalem, and in all Judea and Samaria, and even to the remotest part of the earth."

II.   THE FULFILLMENT

This stream of prophecies and promises found its fulfillment ten days later, on the Day of Pentecost, as recorded in Acts 2. How is this fulfillment understood by those in Pentecostal and Charismatic circles? Primarily in terms of miraculous spiritual gifts, especially the gift of tongues. It is further assumed that these miraculous gifts (especially tongues) are intended for all Christians throughout the church age.

How has this fulfillment been traditionally understood in the Restoration Movement? *Also* in terms of miraculous power, specifically the ability to speak in tongues! It is usually denied, though, that this power was intended for everyone. As a direct outpouring of the Spirit, it is seen as being limited strictly to Pentecost (to either the twelve apostles or to the 120 disciples), with the one later exception of Cornelius and his household as recorded in Acts 10. The Pentecostal blessing is thus exhausted in a one-time event with a single encore.

My thesis here is that *both* of these interpretations are wrong, in that both see miraculous gifts as the essence of the Pentecostal promise. I say this is wrong, mainly because miraculous gifts from the Holy Spirit were NOT a NEW THING, whereas the indwelling presence of the Spirit given in baptism WAS NEW. What God was promising through Isaiah, Ezekiel, Joel, John the Baptist, and Jesus Himself was NOT just the continuation of something that had been present for centuries. It was something profoundly new! It was not just gifts from the Spirit; it was the gift of the Holy Spirit Himself, to dwell within us. See Ezekiel 36:27 and John 7:37-39 again.

A. The Gift of the Spirit

One blessing which Old Testament believers did not enjoy was the indwelling, sanctifying presence of God's Holy Spirit. In those days the Spirit was sent to *equip* certain ones of God's people with such skills and abilities as were necessary for service. See, e.g., Exodus 31:1-5; Numbers 11:17; Judges 3:10; 1 Samuel 16:13. This was only an *external* presence of the Spirit, and was not directly related to the individual's salvation. Even unbelievers could receive it; see 1 Samuel 19:20-24.

What God was promising to give to believers in the new age, however, was the *inward* presence of the Spirit: the indwelling, life-giving, sin-killing, soul-strengthening gift of the Holy Spirit. See 1 Corinthians 6:19; Romans 8:13; Ephesians 3:16; Philippians 2:13. This is the essence of the promise, as Ezekiel 36:27 indicates: "I will put my Spirit within you and cause you to walk in my statutes." Jesus compared it with "rivers of living water" flowing up from within (John 7:38; see Isaiah 43:19-20;

44:3). This is the real Pentecostal power: power to be good, to resist sin, and to witness with boldness.

How is this related to Pentecost? This was the day when this indwelling gift was made available to God's people for the very first time. This was the day the prophecy was fulfilled (Acts 2:16ff.) This was the day when Jesus kept His promise and poured forth the Spirit (Acts 2:33). The Spirit had come! This new gift was now available to all! Thus Peter assured the people that whoever repented and was baptized would receive the gift for his or her very own, "for the promise is for you and your children, and for all who are far off" (Acts 2:38-39; see Acts 5:32).

B.   Not Miraculous Gifts

Of course, there *were* miracles on Pentecost and later, all given by the Holy Spirit. The gift of tongues was prominent among them. But it must be recognized that in His work of equipping God's people for service down through the centuries, the Holy Spirit had already been giving miraculous powers whenever they were needed. We need only to mention Moses and Elijah from the Old Testament. We should remember too that the apostles had already been given miraculous powers long before Pentecost (Matthew 10:1, 8), and so had other disciples (Luke 10:9). To see such powers as the essence of Pentecost does not do justice to the pregnancy of the promise. From the standpoint of the early church it would have been a great let-down, a disappointment something like opening a golden, jeweled chest and finding in it only a few jelly beans. (This let-down is all the more intense when the fulfillment of the promise is limited to only two occasions.)

But again, there *were* miracles on Pentecost! If the gift of tongues was not the essence of the promise, then what *was* the purpose of the tongues-speaking (or prophesying, as Joel calls it; see Acts 2:17-18)? Now, this should not be a difficult question. What is the purpose of *any* miracle? As Scripture plainly teaches, God endowed His servants with miraculous powers whenever there was a revealed message or a truth or a claim to be divinely verified and confirmed. Thus miracles were called *signs*. See Mark 2:10; John 20:30-31; 2 Corinthians 12:12; Hebrews 2:3-4.

This is clearly the main purpose of the gift of tongues on Pentecost. It was a *sign* to everyone, then and now, that this was the day when the new presence of the Holy Spirit was given as promised. It was a sign or evidence for the sake of the audience. Because of this remarkable sign of tongues, no one could doubt that the Spirit had finally come. (Likewise later with Cornelius the tongues were *evidence*—in that case, evidence that the Spirit was intended for Gentiles as well as for Jews. See Acts 10:44-46.)

To see the function of the Pentecostal tongues and to see that they were nothing new, one need only consider the important parallel in Numbers 11:16-30. Here God instructs Moses to choose seventy elders to assist him in leading the Israelites. He specifically says, "I will take of the Spirit who is upon you, and will put Him upon them; and they shall bear the burden of the people with you" (v. 17).

But how could Moses, and the men, and the people in general, know for sure that these men had been marked and empowered by God for special leadership among them? On the appointed day the men gathered at the tabernacle. "Then the LORD ... took of the Spirit who was upon him [Moses] and placed Him upon the seventy elders. And when the Spirit rested upon them, **they prophesied**. But they did not do it again" (v. 25). Here a clear distinction is made between the actual giving of the Spirit (to equip for service), and the miraculous prophesying which served as a *sign* that the deed was done. (Verses 26 & 27 show the miraculous nature of the prophesying, and also show how it was made visible to all the people. See also 1 Samuel 10:6-10; 19:20-24.)

This is exactly the case with Pentecost. There *was* prophesying, as Joel had promised (Joel 2:28; Acts 2:17-18); this was the gift of tongues.

But this was merely incidental and evidential in relation to the *real* gift of Pentecost, the Holy Spirit *Himself!*

We should also note that the purpose of the gift of tongues was NOT to enable the apostles to communicate the *gospel of Christ* to the multinational audience. All the nationalities spoke Greek as the common language; once the miracle had got the people's attention, Peter preached the gospel to all the people in the Greek language. The people's response to the earlier snippets given in their native languages was not repentance and submission to Jesus, but wonder and amazement (Acts 2:7-12)— which is exactly the purpose of a miracle.

In view of these facts I ask: *why should the miraculous manifestations at Pentecost (or with Cornelius) be considered the essence of the new-age outpouring of the Holy Spirit? These things were nothing new!* What *is* the newness of the Spirit's work in the church age? The answer is simple: the *indwelling presence* of the Spirit, for the purpose of spiritual (not miraculous) power. This is the point of all the promises in the prophets and of most of them in the Gospels. The miraculous accompaniments were merely *signs* that this age was beginning. Whether miracles such as tongues continued past the apostolic age or ended there, has nothing to do with either the prophecies or with Pentecost. This question must be settled on other grounds.

THE ESSENCE OF SPIRITUAL GIFTS

The basic principle determining the nature of spiritual gifts is that the Holy Spirit gives ministering gifts according to the NEEDS of the GROUP. Gifts are not given for the recipient's sake, but for the sake of the body of believers as a whole. Such gifts were given among the Israelites in Old Testament times, and they are also given within the church under the New Covenant.

Here are two examples of how the Spirit gave such ministering gifts under the Old Covenant. First is the equipping of the tabernacle craftsmen, the ones chosen to build the tabernacle according to the specifications revealed by God in the Law of Moses in the latter part of Exodus. God explains to Moses how He has prepared the workforce in Exodus 31:1-6:

> The LORD said to Moses, "See, I have called by name Bezalel the son of Uri, son of Hur, of the tribe of Judah, and I have filled him with the Spirit of God, with ability and intelligence, with knowledge and all craftsmanship, to devise artistic designs, to work in gold, silver, and bronze, in cutting stones for setting, and in carving wood, to work in every craft. And behold, I have appointed with him Oholiab, the son of Ahisamach, of the tribe of Dan. And I have given to all able men ability, that they may make all that I have commanded you."

SECTION TWO: MISCELLANEOUS STUDIES ON THE HOLY SPIRIT

See Exodus 35:30 – 36:2 to see how Moses passed this instruction along to the people of Israel.

When we study what God says here about this work of the Holy Spirit, we can learn some important things about the nature of spiritual gifts. Here we will note that in this case, in view of a specific (1) *need*, specific individuals were (2) *called* by God, through Moses to accomplish a certain (3) *task*. Then they were given the (4) *ability* to accomplish the task. Bezalel and Oholiab, the ones in charge, were probably given certain skills outright—the supernatural gift of non-miraculous skills—since they were responsible for the entire project. Others who already had specific skills were called to use them, but God *enhanced* these skills (Exodus 31:6; 36:1).

The craftsmen pooled their gifts to serve the need of the people as a whole. This is according to the principle in 1 Corinthians 12:7; 14:12; 1 Peter 4:10. The main point is that there was a TASK that needed to be done. Abilities were given and dedicated to accomplish the task. This is, I believe, a type for the New Testament church, which is God's tabernacle or temple today (1 Corinthians 3:16-17; 1 Peter 2:5).

The second example of how the Spirit gave ministering gifts within Israel is the selection of seventy assistants to help Moses govern the Israelites during their years of wandering in the wilderness, as recorded in Numbers 11:16ff. The need in this case was for leaders who would be able to help lead and control the rebellious people who were constantly complaining to Moses and overloading him with stress. God's solution is explained in Numbers 11:16-17:

> Then the LORD said to Moses, "Gather for me seventy men of the elders of Israel, whom you know to be the elders of the people and officers over them, and bring them to the tent of meeting, and let them take their stand there with you. And I will come down and talk with you there. And I will take some of the Spirit that is on you and

put it on them, and they shall bear the burden of the people with you, so that you may not bear it yourself alone."

Again we see that Moses was to choose those who already had some leadership experience and ability, and call them to accomplish a specific task because of a specific need. Then God enhanced their skills by filling them with the Holy Spirit for that specific purpose (Numbers 11:24-25).

A point that should be emphasized when we are considering who has what spiritual gifts is this: we must be very careful to differentiate between spiritual gifts and providential gifts. In the context of the church today, *spiritual* gifts are given by the Spirit to Christians to meet the church's needs; *providential* gifts are inborn talents or developed abilities. Providential gifts are present naturally throughout the human population, among Christians and non-Christians alike.

Here is where caution must be taken: just because someone has a natural ability of some kind, such as the ability to speak or the ability to be a leader, such a skill in and of itself is NOT a spiritual gift. Providential gifts should NOT be confused with gifts of the Spirit. An innate ability for teaching or preaching does not automatically qualify someone to be a teacher or preacher *in the church*. Here is an example of a circumstance where this distinction becomes important: a church may have new converts from denominational backgrounds who have obvious teaching or leadership ability, but they may still hold to much of their old denominational theology. Their providential ability to teach or lead is not a *spiritual gift* until they mature in their doctrine (Ephesians 4:11-16), and can be formally approved and *called* by the present church leadership. Another situation where this distinction becomes important is when confronted with the feminist claim that because a woman has a great providential gift for speaking, this qualifies as her spiritual gift and means that she should be accepted as a preacher or elder, despite 1 Timothy 2:12. Remember: providential gifts are not the same as spiritual gifts.

We might note here that so-called "spiritual gift inventories" are often *providential* gift inventories.

What, then, constitutes a spiritual gift? I would include four things. First, the NEED should be considered. Israel needed a portable worship center; Moses needed to reduce his workload. Churches need spiritual leadership; they need teachers; they need oversight for their benevolent programs, among other things.

The second thing is the TASK. Once a need has been identified, then a task or ministry can be designed that will meet that need. This is a primary aspect in the essence of spiritual gifts. It is equivalent to a job description. Exactly what needs to be done to meet the need?

The third thing that qualifies something as a spiritual gift is an official or formal CALLING, usually from the present church leadership. This is an aspect of spiritual gifts that is often overlooked or ignored. Instead, a more common approach is that each individual is exhorted to "discover" his or her "spiritual gift," then volunteer to use it. The result is often a confusion with providential gifts.

In Bible times God often took the initiative and directly called specific individuals to fill specific roles, e.g., Moses and Paul. He also called Bezalel and Oholiab to lead the tabernacle project. But most of the time, God calls *indirectly,* through the ones who are already in leadership roles. E.g., Moses was in charge of seeking out the best tribal leaders to be his seventy assistants. In Acts 6 the apostles instructed the church itself to select seven men to oversee their benevolent program. The point is that one does not have a *spiritual gift* until *called* by the church to fulfill a task.

Also, this shows that we should not wait until someone volunteers. If there is a need, the church should seek out the best qualified and call them to serve, anointing them and praying for them and expecting the Holy Spirit to enable them (see Acts 6:6).

The fourth thing that is included in a spiritual gift is ABILITY. Where does ability fit in? Some may think this is the first or most important aspect. The fact is that it is the least significant of these four elements. This is very important: what many think are "spiritual gifts" are not! They are often providential gifts, either innate or developed. Just because someone has a "natural" ability is not in itself equivalent to a spiritual gift. It may indeed qualify one to be *called* to a particular task, and should be taken into consideration; but this alone is not decisive. If one discerns a providential gift, he or she should dedicate it to the Lord's work and let the church leadership know of this willingness to serve.

Here are some principles for applying the above data in this age of the church:

1. Spiritual gifts are based primarily on need, not on ability as such.

2. Church leaders are responsible for getting individual Christians involved, first by identifying needs and therefore delineating tasks or ministries to meet them; and then by calling individuals to fulfill these tasks. Here, abilities must be taken into account (see Exodus 31:6; Numbers 11:16), but this is not the main point.

3. Each individual must be *aware* of his or her providential gifts, and must consecrate these gifts to the Master's use. But even more importantly, each one must consecrate ONESELF to ANY service to which one may be called by the church. See Acts 6:3. Here it is not stated that these seven men had some special aptitude for benevolent work, but they were willing and available for whatever task the church called them to.

4. Finally, the church must NOT call individuals to fill specific roles or work at certain tasks contrary to the stated will of the Holy Spirit, no matter what providential gifts may be present. For example, in Numbers 11:16, seventy *men* are specified; in Acts 6:3, seven *men* are specified.

DOES THE SPIRIT GIVE MIRACULOUS GIFTS TODAY? A STUDY OF 1 CORINTHIANS 13:8-13

One of the most serious and most divisive issues facing Christendom today is whether or not the Holy Spirit still gives gifts involving supernatural or miraculous powers to Christians in the post-apostolic era. This issue has been argued down through Christian history, but has become especially critical in the twentieth century and after, with the rise of Pentecostalism, the Charismatic Movement, and the more recent "third wave" of the Holy Spirit. Especially within these circles it is believed that the Spirit is giving the same gifts of prophecy, tongues, healing, and other miracles that were given in the church's first generation as recorded in the New Testament. Others take a "cessationist" view, arguing that such gifts ceased being given once the last apostle died.

I am a firm believer is the cessationist view, and have so argued and taught throughout my teaching career. I defended this view in my seminary course on the Holy Spirit, and I have explained the case for it in both of my College Press books on the Holy Spirit: *The Holy Spirit: A Biblical Study* (2006, 131pp., pb), and *Power from on High: What the Bible Says About the Holy Spirit* (2007, 506pp., hb). In my seminary course I presented as many as six arguments that show why the Spirit is not giving miraculous gifts today. In this essay I will name the first five and go into detail on the sixth, drawing my material from the seminary course outline.

The first five lines of evidence are these. (1) The purpose of miracles in general limits them to the time when new revelation concerning new redemptive works is being given. No such redemptive works have been performed and explained via revelation since the first century. (2) The main purpose of the Pentecostal outpouring of the Spirit in Acts 2 was NOT to begin a new era of miraculous gifts. Rather, it was to inaugurate the saving work of the *indwelling* of the Spirit. (3) The purpose of the new "baptism in the Holy Spirit" was the same. Being baptized in the Spirit is another way of describing the reception of the indwelling of the Spirit in Christian baptism. (4) The purpose of spiritual gifts as such was and is to meet the existing needs of the church at the time. Miraculous gifts were needed only in the foundational era of the church. (5) There is a necessary connection between the reception of miraculous gifts and the apostolic laying-on-of-hands, but the apostles were all gone by the end of the first century. (See the books mentioned above for a full explanation of these points.)

The main reason for rejecting the idea that miraculous gifts from the Spirit have continued beyond the apostolic age is that the New Testament contains a specific statement to the effect that (at least certain) miraculous gifts have ceased. I am speaking of 1 Corinthians 13:10, as it appears in its full context of 1 Corinthians 13:8-13 as follows (from the New Revised Standard Version):

> [8] Love never ends. But as for prophecies, they will come to an end; as for tongues, they will cease; as for knowledge, it will come to an end. [9] For we know only in part, and we prophesy only in part; [10] but when the complete comes, the partial will come to an end. [11] When I was a child, I spoke like a child, I thought like a child, I reasoned like a child; when I became an adult, I put an end to childish ways. [12] For now we see in a mirror, dimly, but then we will see face to face. Now I know only in part; then I will know fully, even as I

have been fully known. [13] And now faith, hope, and love abide, these three; and the greatest of these is love.

The key verse is verse 10: "But when the complete comes, the partial will come to an end."

Some have argued that all the spiritual gifts named in the New Testament are continuing throughout Christian history. This assumption is shown to be false by the nature of the gift of apostles (Ephesians 4:11; 1 Corinthians 12:28-29). It is almost universally accepted that the gift of apostleship was temporary. This shows that it is possible that some other gifts might also be temporary. Indeed, we see that 1 Corinthians 13:8-13 affirms that this is actually the case.

The structure of this passage is very important. It contains two distinct contrasts. The main contrast is between things that are *temporary* (verse 8: tongues, prophecy, and knowledge), and things that are *permanent* (verse 13: faith, hope, and love). The things in the latter group were already present when Paul was writing, and it is affirmed that they will continue.

The second contrast, in verses 9-12, is very important. It shows WHY the gifts mentioned in verse 8 are only temporary. (This is a kind of parenthesis between verses 8 and 13.) The irony is that the very things the Corinthians prized most highly were only temporary. WHY were they temporary? Because they were only *partial*, i.e., composed of bits and pieces. Because they were only partial, they were never intended to be permanent, but were intended to be replaced by something that is *complete*: "But when the complete thing comes, the partial will be done away" (v. 10).

The key word here is *teleion*, an adjective which means "perfect, mature, complete." Most translations of the New Testament render this word as "perfect" in this verse. That translation is indefensible, and has been a main part of the faulty case for continuing miraculous gifts. Using the translation "perfect," it has been further assumed that this is a reference to the only perfect *person*, namely, Jesus Christ; and since it refers to the time when the "perfect comes," it is seen as referring to the second coming of Jesus. The conclusion, then, is that gifts such as prophecy, tongues, and miraculous knowledge (see vv. 1-2) will continue until the second coming of Jesus. This disastrous interpretation is contrary to everything verse 10 is saying.

It should be clear from the beginning that *teleion* is not intended to mean "perfect" here, because of the obvious contrast with that which is *partial.* This contrast shows that the translation of *teleion* should be "complete." On the "Bible Gateway" website, I checked how their 59 Bible versions translated *teleion.* Sixteen correctly translated it "complete"; three versions put "complete and perfect"; the remaining two-thirds still say "the perfect," or "that which is perfect," or "perfection." Using this "perfect" translation is inexcusable and misleading, in view of the contrast with "partial."

Also, it is important to note that this adjective *teleion* is in the neuter form; thus it should be translated as "the complete *thing.*" It does NOT refer to a person, such as Jesus Christ. It is *not* a reference to Jesus at His second coming.

Thus the main point of the statement in verse ten is this: when the complete thing comes, the partial and temporary things will CEASE! We should note that there is a temporal and logical connection between the coming of the complete thing and the cessation of the partial things. WHEN the complete thing comes, the partial will come to an end. The Greek construction is *hotan* with the subjunctive case, which means that the *teleion* will come before the cessation of these gifts and will be the condition for it. (See Arndt and Gingrich's Greek-English lexicon, 1952 edition, p. 592.) What this shows is that one cannot be a cessationist and at the same time try to link the *teleion* with the second coming of Jesus.

Coming to the main point, we now ask – what is the *complete thing*, the *teleion*? From the text itself we can determine some limitations as to the time when it will appear, thus narrowing down the possibilities. For one thing, the *teleion* will come AFTER Paul wrote 1 Corinthians, naturally. Verse ten uses future tense and is pointing to a future event. This rules out "love" as the complete thing, since love was already present in the church when Paul wrote this. Also, the text shows that the *teleion* must come BEFORE the eschaton, i.e., before the end of the age and the second coming of Jesus. We see this in verse 13, which says that the temporary, partial things will cease while faith, hope, and love are *still abiding*. But by its very nature, *hope* will no longer be present after the second coming; it will be obsolete when we actually have the things for which we have been hoping (see Romans 8:24-25). Thus the complete thing must appear *before* the end of the age, not AT the end. This rules out all eschatological interpretations of the *teleion*.

In the second place, the text helps us to determine the identity of the *teleion* by telling us what things it is in contrast with, i.e., what sorts of things it will be replacing. The contrast says the complete thing will take the place of the partial things. This indicates that the complete thing will be *the same kind of thing* as the partial things that it will replace. So, what do the gifts of prophecy, tongues, and miraculous knowledge have in common? What sort of thing must the *teleion* be that it may take the place of these? The answer is that the prophecy, tongues, and knowledge all belong to the category of *revealed knowledge*. Thus we conclude that the *teleion* itself will be in the category of *revealed knowledge*. Yet it will be *complete*, in contrast with these partial forms. (This consideration also rules out love as the "complete thing." Likewise it rules out the view that the "complete thing" is the mature church itself. Neither of these is in the category of revealed knowledge and thus is not appropriate as a replacement for the items in verse 8.)

The only thing that satisfies all the requirements is that the *teleion* must be *the completed New Testament*. Christians under the New Covenant would certainly *expect* such a completed testament, similar to the Old Testament that had been given for those under the Old Covenant. We should note that Christians were already equating apostolic writings with Scripture: 1 Timothy 5:18; 2 Peter 3:15-16. Also, God's will and word under the New Covenant are described as *teleios* in other places in the New Testament: Romans 12:2; James 1:25; Hebrew 5:14; 6:1.

Before we can close this discussion, we must give close attention to 1 Corinthians 13:12. I have said above that we cannot interpret the *teleion* as something that occurs in connection with the second coming of Christ. But verse 12, as usually translated, seems to put it into that context, which would then be inconsistent with the idea that the *teleion* is the completed New Testament. Here is a familiar translation of verse 12: "For now we see in a mirror dimly, but then face to face; now I know in part, but then I will know fully just as I also have been fully known" (NASB). Many assume that this verse is saying that the contrast between the partial and the complete is a contrast between this present church age and the heavenly state that follows the second coming. This, however, is a false understanding of this verse, especially of the phrase "face to face"—as I will now explain.

First, we shall consider this part of the verse: "For now we see in a mirror dimly, but then face to face." Here is the Greek for this: *blepomen gar arti di' esoptrou en ainigmati, tote de prosōpon pros prosōpon*. The contrast is usually thought to be between "seeing in a mirror dimly" and "seeing face to face." The "face to face" seeing is taken to mean seeing *Jesus* face to face, after the second coming.

But this is not the idea at all. The contrast is between "seeing **in a mirror** *DIMLY*," and "*seeing* **in a mirror** face to face," or CLEARLY. The "seeing in a mirror" applies to both sides of the contrast; the difference is that one mirror is of poor quality and the other is bright, shiny, and clear.

Thus the point is that both sides are referring to forms of *revelation* (revealed knowledge), the latter being superior to the former. The former ("dimly") represents enigmatic, incomplete revelation; the latter ("face to face") represents clear, complete revelation. Both occur within history, prior to the eschaton.

The key to this understanding is the Greek phrase *en ainigmati*, translated "dimly." Literally it means "in a riddle." (I *seriously* recommend that everyone read the article on the word *ainigma*, "riddle," in Kittel's *Theological Dictionary of the New Testament* [TDNT], I:178ff.) When we follow the trail of the word *ainigma*, it leads us to the Greek Septuagint translation of the Old Testament (the LXX), in Numbers 12:8. Here Yahweh is explaining to Aaron and Miriam the difference between the way He usually spoke to Moses, in contrast with the way He spoke to most prophets. "With him [Moses] I speak mouth to mouth, clearly, and not in riddles." The phrase "mouth to mouth" is equivalent to "face to face" in 1 Corinthians 13:12; and "in riddles" is the same as "dimly" in 13:12. What we see here is that the apostle Paul is using the language of Numbers 12:8 to contrast the partial and the complete in 1 Corinthians 13. And the contrast in both cases is between *two kinds of revelation*: the less clear, and the more clear. It has nothing to do with an alleged heavenly form of speaking as distinct from a this-age revelation.

Even the idea of "seeing in a mirror" should be understood in terms of the Rabbinic reflections on Numbers 12:8. First, we must certainly reject the idea that Paul is talking about seeing "through a window" at all, whether dimly or clearly. The reference is to seeing "in a mirror." According to the article cited above from Kittel's TDNT, this concept comes from an idea common in Rabbinic literature, i.e., depicting *revelation* in terms of occultish mirror-gazing or crystal-ball gazing. This is by no means an endorsement of such a practice, but we should note that in reference to Numbers 12:8 the Rabbis said that Moses saw God in a *clear* mirror, while other prophets saw Him in a *cloudy* mirror (TDNT,

I:178). As applied to 1 Corinthians 13:12, the distinction is *not* between
(1) seeing ONLY in a mirror—all ancient mirrors being cloudy by nature,
and (2) seeing IN PERSON. This is not the point. Rather, the distinction
is between (1) seeing in a cloudy mirror, and (2) seeing in a *clear* mirror—
which *were* available in Paul's day, contrary to a popular myth. See TDNT,
I:179. The point is simply that the present gifts of prophecy, tongues, and
knowledge were like looking into the cloudy mirror; whereas using the
coming *teleion* would be like looking into a clear mirror.

We should also note that the text does not say that when we look into
the clear mirror, we shall "see HIM face to face." There is no "him," and
no object at all. The expression "see face to face" is not about *whom* we will
see, but *how* we will be seeing once the *teleion* comes. The expression refers
to the *kind* of seeing, namely, to the clarity of the revelation. It will be as
clear as seeing one's face in a sharp and clear mirror. (See Numbers 12:8;
Genesis 32:30; Judges 6:22; Deuteronomy 34:10.) Incidentally, the Greek
expression for seeing another person "face to face" was *kata prosōpon*, as in
Acts 25:16; 2 Corinthians 10:1, 7; Galatians 2:11, not the expression in
our text, *prosōpon pros prosōpon*. See the article on *prosōpon* in Kittel,
TDNT, VI:768-779.

This is not the only New Testament reference to "looking in a
mirror," and the other such references to "looking in a mirror" and seeing
clearly refer to looking into the Word of God in the form of the New
Testament. See 2 Corinthians 3:7ff. (verse 18 specifically) and James 1:23-
25. In 2 Corinthians 3:18 especially, the comparison is between the Old
Covenant Scriptures, the reading of which is like looking through a veil,
and the New Covenant Scriptures, the reading of which is like seeing
Christ without a veil, i..e., face to face. The point is that we do not have
to wait until the second coming to see Christ, as it were, "face to face." See
TDNT, VI:776. Also, 2 Corinthians 4:6 refers to seeing the face of Christ
in the gospel. The comparison with 1 Corinthians 13:12 is obvious. The

piece-meal revelations (tongues, prophecy) are to the completed New Testament what the Old Testament is to the New Testament.

Here is an extended paraphrase of the first part of 1 Corinthians 13:12 – "For now, while we depend on occasional revelations through prophecy or interpreted tongues, it is like trying to see yourself in a scratched and cloudy mirror. But then, when the completed New Testament has been given, it will be like seeing a sharp, clear image of yourself in a bright new mirror."

We now turn to the second statement in verse 12, "Now I know in part, but then I shall know fully just as I also have been fully known." The Greek is this: *arti ginōskō ek merous, tote de epignōsomai kathōs kai epegnōthēn*. The issue is that two different words for "to know" are used here: *ginōskō* in the first clause, and *epiginōskō* in the second. Some think that the second word refers to a kind of knowledge that will be possible only after Jesus comes. This, however, is another myth. The knowledge of which Paul here speaks (in the second clause) is *not* some kind of special, eschatological knowledge available only in heaven.

The two verbs for "to know" as used here are *ginōskō*, and the same word with the preposition *epi* added. It is simply assumed by many that adding *epi* somehow converts this into a "knowing" that is qualitatively different from the other. But contrary to this popular belief, *epiginōskō* does not necessarily carry any stronger meaning than *ginōskō*. There is no warrant for translating it as "know *fully* as opposed to just "know." Consider the following comparisons and bits of data:

- Matthew 7:16, 20 says that we human beings shall know (*epiginōskō*) them by their fruits, but in Matthew 7:23 Jesus says, "I never knew you" (*ginōskō*). If *epignōskō* is the stronger word, we would have expected it in verse 23.

- In Matthew 11:27 the Father's knowledge of the Son and the Son's knowledge of the Father are described with the term *epiginōskō*. But in John 10:15 the same knowledge is given as *ginōskō*. In fact, John never uses *epiginōskō*.

- See the interchangeable use in Luke 24:16, 31 (*epiginōskō*) and Luke 24:35 (*ginōskō*).

- The term *epiginōskō* IS used of some very extraordinary events, but also of some very ordinary ones, e.g., Acts 12:14; 19:34; 28:1.

- Both *epiginōskō* (verb) and *epignōsis* (noun) are used extensively of present knowledge of God's truth. See 2 Corinthians 1:13; 1 Timothy 4:3; 2 Peter 2:21; Ephesians 1:17; 4:13; Colossians 1:9; 1 Timothy 2:4; 2 Timothy 2:25; 3:7; Titus 1:1; Hebrews 10:26.

- Apart from the passage that is the point of disagreement here (1 Corinthians 13:12), neither *epiginōskō* or *epignōsis* is used of any kind of eschatological knowledge.

- *The New International Dictionary of New Testament Theology*, in its article on "knowledge," does not even mention any kind of distinction between *ginōskō* and *epiginōskō*.

- The article on these words in Kittel's TDNT says they are used "interchangeably" in the New Testament and "with no difference in meaning" (I:703). "That there is no general distinction between the simple and compound forms in early Christian writings is shown by a comparison of Mk. 2:8 with 8:17; Mk. 5:30 with Lk. 8:46; Mk. 6:33,54 with Lk. 9:11; Mt. 7:16,20 with Lk. 6:44; Mt. 11:27 with Lk. 10:22; Lk. 24:31 with 24:35; Colossians 1:6 with 2 C. 8:9.... Even in 1 C. 13:12 the alternation is purely rhetorical" (I:704). Note: **the alternation is purely rhetorical!**

In 1 Corinthians 13:12 the *object* of the knowledge is not given. It does not say that we shall know *God* as fully as He knows us. This would be blasphemous to say. It is not necessarily a reference to knowledge of God or Christ at all. It may mean simply that we shall know *ourselves* with more clarity, or know what we *ought* to be in a clearer way as revealed through the Bible (cf. Hebrews 4:12; 2 Timothy 3:16; James 1:23-25).

All thoughts of *full* knowledge or omniscience should be put out of our minds altogether. Omniscience belongs to God alone. Such knowledge is impossible for us because we are finite creatures and can never be anything else. Not even in heaven will we have unlimited knowledge either of God or of ourselves. Our knowledge at any stage can only be *relatively* "full" or "complete," as compared with what has gone before. When the church received the completed New Testament, its knowledge could be called "complete" only as compared with the partial knowledge given via the temporary spiritual gifts.

The conclusion is that 1 Corinthians 13:12 is not necessarily speaking of any kind of eschatological knowledge that will be ours only when we are glorified or only when we get to heaven or only when Jesus comes again. The statements made in this verse are quite consistent with the interpretation of the *teleion* in verse 10 as the completed New Testament, which gives us a body of knowledge that is relatively clear and complete when compared with the fragments of knowledge given in the earliest days of the church via miraculous spiritual gifts.

We conclude, then, that by far, the best understanding of 1 Corinthians 13:10 is that it refers to the completed New Testament. In addition to the five arguments listed at the beginning of this essay, this is a very strong argument in support of the fact that miraculous gifts ceased being passed along after the death of the apostles.

ADDENDUM
MISCELLANEOUS ARGUMENTS FOR CESSATIONISM

In addition to the above, the following are a few more considerations that help to support the view called cessationism.

First, those whose theological systems are built around a belief in the continuation of miraculous gifts, such as the Charismatic Movement and the Word of Faith movement, tend to elevate experience above the Word of God as the basis for their beliefs. For more data on this, see the works by John MacArthur called *Charismatic Chaos* and *Strange Fire*. Such an appeal to experience is invalid and deceiving; see Matthew 7:21-23; Luke 13:25-28.

Second, in these contexts the Holy Spirit is often elevated above Jesus Christ, contrary to the Spirit's stated mission. See John 16:14-15.

Third, the miraculous manifestations today occur in conjunction with all kinds of false doctrines and false religions, thus creating a false unity. Here is an observation by Kurt Koch, an Evangelical who had considerable experience working with those involved in occult practices: "In America, Jesuits, Lutherans, free church people, modern theologians, High Anglicans, and Mormons meet together in order to speak in tongues. They are convinced that this is true Ecumenicalism in action. This sounds fantastic. And yet I heard of a similar group in London." Then Koch continues sarcastically, "What a wonderful time we live in today! All schisms, all denominational barriers, age-long divisions have been overcome by the new gift of tongues. Does this really mean that what the Word of God could not accomplish, has been brought about by a psychic epidemic?" (*The Strife of Tongues*, p. 25).

Fourth, despite the false unity just mentioned, the presence of such "miraculous spiritual gifts" actually tends to divide the Lord's people and the Lord's churches, contrary to the uniting purpose of the Spirit.

Fifth, modern tongue-speakers usually do not adhere to the Biblical "rules" for speaking in tongues. Based on his observations of Charismatic worship services, Kurt Koch (ibid., p. 39) makes the following comments related to the Biblical passages listed. Regarding 1 Corinthians 14:34: "Women are not to speak publicly in tongues. This is not heeded anywhere in the new tongues movement." Regarding 1 Corinthians 14:27: "Only two or three should speak in tongues on any one occasion. No notice is taken of this either in the new tongues movement. Ten, twenty or even more people speak in tongues at the same prayer meeting." Regarding 1 Corinthians 14:1, 39: "The gift of tongues is called the lowest gift by Paul, but today it is given first place in the tongues movement."

Sixth, some say that even Paul seems to have been unable to perform healing miracles at the end of his ministry. The evidence for this would be the workers who helped Paul but who are mentioned as being sick, namely, Epaphroditus, Philippians 2:25ff.; Timothy, 1 Timothy 5:23; and Trophimus, 2 Timothy 4:20. These are men Paul failed to heal, though it would have been to Paul's advantage to have healed them.

THE HOLY SPIRIT IN ACTS 8:4-25

QUESTION: As Philip evangelized the Samaritans, many believed and were baptized (Acts 8:12). But verses 15-17 seem to say that the converts did not receive the Holy Spirit at their baptism, but rather when apostles from Jerusalem came and laid hands on them. Other texts also separate the receiving of the Spirit from baptism (e.g., Acts 10:44-48). How can we explain this, especially in light of Acts 2:38?

ANSWER: All Zwinglians—those who separate baptism from salvation—love to call attention to such data from the book of Acts. They believe that these data show that there is no appointed connection between baptism and the gift of the Holy Spirit. The fallacy in this interpretation is the assumption that every "receiving" of the Holy Spirit (e.g., Acts 8:15-17) is in some sense for the purpose of salvation. This assumption is false, and it usually contributes to a false doctrine of baptism and salvation.

The fact is that in the book of Acts we can identify at least THREE different ways in which the Holy Spirit is given and received, each for a distinctly different purpose, and each to bestow a different kind of gift. All three of these ways, purposes, and gifts are found in the second chapter of Acts. I sometimes call them (1) SIGN gifts, (2) TRUTH gifts, and (3) SALVATION gifts. (We could add SERVICE gifts to this list, but these are not very prominent in Acts, especially in Acts 2. Thus we will just focus here on three kinds of gifts.)

SECTION TWO: MISCELLANEOUS STUDIES ON
THE HOLY SPIRIT

In Acts 2:1-13, the first way the Holy Spirit came upon individuals was to bestow SIGN gifts, specifically "speaking in tongues," or the ability to speak fluently in a language one has never studied. Many have wrongly been taught and have wrongly assumed that the purpose of the tongue-speaking was to preach the gospel of Jesus Christ to all the nationalities present. There is nothing in the text to support this idea. The only reference to the content of the tongue-speaking is in verse 11, which says they proclaimed "the mighty works of God." The best inference is that these "mighty works" were the great events of deliverance and redemption recorded in the Old Testament—things this Jewish audience would immediately identify with.

This is not a problem, since the purpose for the tongue-speaking was not its content, but its form. It was a MIRACLE, the main purpose of which is always to provide divinely-given proof (evidence, confirmation) of accompanying REVELATION. In this case the tongue-speaking was proof of the truth of Peter's sermon, which immediately follows (2:14ff.). As such, this kind of outpouring of the Spirit was nothing new; the Spirit had been coming upon certain individuals to provide them with miracle-working power at least since the time of Moses. Jesus Himself had the Spirit upon Him for this purpose (see Luke 4:14; Acts 10:38), and the apostles had already experienced it during Jesus' ministry (Matthew 10:1ff.).

We should emphasize that there is no connection between receiving a sign gift and receiving salvation. Most often those who received gifts were already saved. Events in the life of Balaam (Numbers 22-24) show that the Spirit could miraculously speak through an unsaved person (24:2; cf. 22:28-30). The fact that Jesus received the Spirit for this purpose definitely shows it was not a salvation thing. The filling of the Holy Spirit for tongue-speaking on Pentecost (Acts 2:4) did not involve salvation.

The second way the Spirit came on individuals is in Acts 2:14ff., when He bestowed TRUTH gifts upon the Apostle Peter. Sometimes we forget that Jesus had promised the apostles that after He was gone He would send the Holy Spirit to them for the purpose of enabling them to speak inspired messages from God (John 14:26; 16:12-15). In this case it was promised that the Spirit would come upon the apostles with the gifts of revelation and inspiration. This is totally distinct from salvation as such.

Acts 2:14 does not specifically say that Peter was inspired by the Holy Spirit as he preached his Pentecost sermon, but we can reasonably infer that this was when Jesus kept His promises as recorded in John 14 and 16. The content of Peter's sermon was not something Peter would already know; it was probably not something that Jesus had already taught the apostles (see John 16:12). Thus Peter is speaking here through the Spirit's gifts of revelation and inspiration. Other Spirit-inspired apostolic teaching is recorded throughout the book of Acts.

The third way the Spirit came on individuals in the second chapter of Acts is seen in 2:37-41; in this case it was to bestow SALVATION gifts. This was indeed the main point of the Pentecostal work of the Spirit. The sign-gift (tongues) and the inspiration-gift (Peter's sermon) were just laying the foundation and paving the way for the SAVING outpouring of the Spirit. This kind of Spirit presence was not given to Old Testament saints, but was prophesied by the Old Testament, by John the Baptist, and by Jesus Himself as a new work that would be the hallmark of the New Covenant era (Isaiah 43:19-20; 44:3-4; Ezekiel 36:27; Joel 2:28-32; Matthew 3:11; John 7:37-39). Those who received the Holy Spirit in the manner described in Acts 2:38 received from Him the salvation gifts of regeneration and sanctification.

Acts 2:38 makes it clear that this third way of receiving the Holy Spirit was a salvation event, being accompanied by the forgiveness of sins. Acts 5:32 refers to "the Holy Spirit, whom God has given to those who obey him." This must be a reference to this third way of receiving the Spirit, because this is the only one for which obedience to conditions is specified. Obedience for this purpose is called "obeying the faith" (Acts

6:7) and "obedience to the gospel" (Romans 10:16; 2 Thessalonians 1:8).
Peter's statement in 5:32 shows that in the post-Pentecost church it was
simply assumed that baptism was the time when the Spirit was given for
salvation purposes; this did not have to be stated again every time a
conversion and baptism were recorded.

How does all this apply to Acts 8:4-25? First, based on the last two
paragraphs above, it is a more than reasonable inference that the
Samaritans who were baptized (vv. 12-13) received the saving presence of
the Spirit in that moment. That this is not specifically stated does not
mean it did not happen. There is no reference to their sins being forgiven,
either; but we rightly assume that it happened, based on the promise in
Acts 2:38.

Now, back to the question about Acts 8:4-25. So why does 8:14-18
say that Phillip's baptized converts had not yet received the Holy Spirit,
and that the visitation by the apostles, Peter and John, actually brought
this about? Because what Peter and John accomplished by laying hands on
the Samaritans was NOT the SALVATION gift of the Spirit, but SIGN
and TRUTH gifts. The latter are totally different from the saving
indwelling of the Spirit. The point was that the Samaritan Christians,
though they had received full salvation (including the Spirit's saving
indwelling) at their baptism, had not received any sign or truth gifts that
could be used in connection with evangelism and edification after Philip
left.

What was accomplished by the laying on the apostles' hands was the
transfer of miracle-working power (sign-gifts such as tongues and healing)
and the ability to prophesy (the truth-gift of being able to speak inspired
messages from God). Though the Spirit was given for a similar purpose to
the apostles in Acts 2, because that was a special event no "laying on of
hands" was used. This bestowal without hands happened only one other
time, as Peter preached to Cornelius and his household, in Acts 10:44-48;
11:15. Other than Pentecost and Cornelius—two special and unique

events, the Spirit gave sign and truth gifts only through the laying on of apostles' hands. See Acts 6:6; 8:17; 19:6.

In Acts 8, how do we know that the result of the laying on of apostles' hands was the reception of sign and/or truth gifts, rather than the saving gift of the Spirit? Because of Simon the Sorcerer's reaction to the result of this laying on of hands. The result was something he could SEE (v. 18), and something spectacular enough to tempt him to fall back into his witchcraft mentality (v. 18-19).

Thus the key to harmonizing the references to the Holy Spirit in the book of Acts is to see that He comes upon people for different purposes.

THE HOLY SPIRIT AND CORNELIUS IN ACTS 10-11

QUESTION: I am confused about the various references to the working of the Holy Spirit in the Book of Acts. E.g., do Acts 1:5 and 1:8 refer to the same work of the Spirit? Is the promise in 1:5 fulfilled in 2:4? Does 11:15-16 tie 1:5 and 2:4 together?

ANSWER: One source of such confusion is the assumption that all works of the Holy Spirit are basically the same. Some add to this the assumption that all works of the Spirit involve salvation. I will try to clear up such confusion by first distinguishing four kinds of gifts bestowed upon individuals by the Spirit.

The first kind of gifts given by the Spirit can be called TRUTH gifts. These involve the Spirit's work of revelation and inspiration, by which the Spirit reveals truth to chosen individuals (usually prophets and apostles), and by which He protects the spoken and written communication of such revelation (and of other truths) from errors and omissions. Such gifts were given in Old Testament times to the prophets of Israel, such as Moses, Elijah, David, Isaiah, and Malachi. Jesus's promise that He would give the Holy Spirit to the apostles for this same purpose is recorded in John 14:26 and 16:12-15. Jesus renews this promise in Acts 1:8, and it began to be fulfilled in Acts 2:14ff. in Peter's Pentecost sermon. The Holy Spirit also later bestowed truth gifts on other Christians, in gifts such as prophecy, knowledge, distinguishing of Spirits, and interpretation of tongues (see 1 Corinthians 12:8-11).

The second kind of gifts given by the Spirit are SIGN gifts. These are supernatural powers that enable a recipient to perform miracles, which function as *signs* (evidence, proof, confirmation) of the divine source and validity of the content given through the truth gifts. Sign gifts were also given in Old Testament times to men such as Moses, Moses's 70 elders (Numbers 11:25), Elijah, and the apostles (Matthew 10:1). Truth gifts and sign gifts almost always go together, since the purpose of the latter us to verify the divine source of the former. Thus it is likely that Jesus is including the promise of sign gifts in Acts 1:8, especially the gift of tongues that was directly given to the apostles beginning in Acts 2:4. The purpose of the miraculous ability to speak in unlearned languages was not to communicate some new data, but to provide a divinely-given sign for the truth of Peter's imminent sermon. The same is true for the divinely-given tongue-speaking ability of Cornelius and his household; it was a divine sign giving proof to the Jews that God desired to save the Gentiles. The Spirit also gave sign gifts to other Christian individuals via the laying on of apostles' hands as the church grew and spread.

The third kind of gifts given by the Spirit are SERVICE gifts, which are abilities and tasks given to individuals to enable them to meet the general needs of God's people as a whole. This is what we usually call "spiritual gifts," but I am including here only those gifts that do not involve prophecy and miracles. The Spirit was giving this kind of gift in Old Testament times (e.g., Exodus 31:1-11), and he still gives them today. These service gifts, as defined here, do not appear in Acts 2.

The fourth kind of gift bestowed by the Spirit is SALVATION gifts, received through the indwelling Holy Spirit as given for the first time on Pentecost in Christian baptism (Acts 2:38). This was a new thing (Isaiah 43:19), not given to Old Testament saints. But now, since Pentecost, every sinner who believes and obeys the gospel receives from the indwelling

Spirit the saving gifts of regeneration (new birth) and sanctification. The beginning of this saving work of the Spirit was one of the main purposes of Pentecost. The miracle of tongues (a sign gift) was given solely as divine proof that this was the day when the Spirit was beginning to give salvation gifts.

Thus we see that on the day of Pentecost as described in Acts 2, three different kinds of the Spirit's work were present: *sign* gifts (vv. 1-13), *truth* gifts (vv. 14-36), and *salvation* gifts (vv. 37-42).

Now I will tie all of this back into Acts 1. I have said that Acts 1:8 probably refers to the truth gifts and sign gifts, in that it promises the apostles that the Holy Spirit will give them power to witness for Jesus. This power is seen especially in the tongues, and the witness is seen mainly in Peter's sermon.

But what about Acts 1:5, where Jesus says John the Baptist's promise that "you will be baptized in the Holy Spirit" was going to occur "not many days from now"? Here is a point many have misunderstood: baptism in the Holy Spirit is *not* a sign gift, and it does not produce miraculous powers such as speaking in tongues. I.e., baptism in the Spirit is not what occurred in Acts 2:1-13. Rather, baptism in the Holy Spirit is another way of describing the SALVATION work of the Spirit which happens to all sinners in the moment of water baptism (see 1 Corinthians 6:11; 12:13). When Jesus made this promise in 1:5 he was not referring to the events of 2:1-13 but to the new thing in 2:38-39. *This* is the Father's promise of the Holy Spirit (2:33, 39); this is what the Day of Pentecost was all about.

How does this relate, then, to the experience of Cornelius and his household (Acts 10:44-48), especially as explained by Peter in Acts 11:15-16? First, in 11:15 Peter reports that "the Holy Spirit fell upon them just as He did upon us at the beginning." Here, "at the beginning" obviously refers to Pentecost (2:1-13). Also, "upon us" refers to the apostles. The phrase "just as" means that the Spirit came upon them in the very same way He came upon the apostles on Pentecost, namely, by a direct outpouring, rather than through any human mediator (such as through the laying on of hands). That puts these two events in a category by themselves. The whole point of Cornelius's display of tongue-speaking was that the Spirit was giving a SIGN gift in order to divinely demonstrate that God did indeed want the Gentiles to be saved, i.e., to receive the SALVATION gifts included in Holy Spirit baptism.

This leads Peter to say what he did in 11:16, "And I remembered the word of the Lord, how He used to say, 'John baptized with water, but you will be baptized with the Holy Spirit.'" Most have assumed that Peter is here identifying baptism in the Holy Spirit with the tongue-speaking he had witnessed in Cornelius' house. I disagree. In 10:47 we see that the first thing Peter concluded upon hearing the tongues was this: "Surely no one can refuse the water for these to be baptized who have received the Holy Spirit just as we did, can he?" Then Acts 11:16 is Peter's own commentary on this; and as I see it, this is what he is saying in 11:16: "As soon as I saw and heard what was happening, I was absolutely convinced that God wants these Gentiles to be saved, i.e., that he wants *them* to receive the baptism in the Spirit also. Thus I immediately said, 'Surely no one can refuse the water for these to be baptized, can they?' After all, they received the miraculous outpouring of the Holy Spirit just as we did on Pentecost. God is surely trying to tell us something, and it is that he wants these and other Gentiles to be saved. So let's get them to the water so they can be baptized in the Holy Spirit! We cannot stand in the way of God and refuse them this gift!"

In other words, Peter's statement in 11:16 is not *backward* looking, referring to the tongue-speaking that had just happened; it is *forward* looking, referring to what must happen next. The *sign* gift (speaking in tongues) was proof that the Gentiles were supposed to receive the *salvation* gifts that would come when they were baptized in the Spirit.

THE HOLY SPIRIT AND PSALMS 51:11

QUESTION: How did King David receive the Holy Spirit?

ANSWER: This question is probably suggested by Psalms 51:11, where David as king prays to God, "Do not take Your Holy Spirit from me." This indicates that when he is saying this prayer, he does have the Holy Spirit in some way. How did he receive the Spirit in the first place?

We must understand that in the Bible people can "have the Holy Spirit" in two very different ways. On the one hand, we may speak of the EQUIPPING presence of the Holy Spirit. This means that some people have received the Holy Spirit for the purpose of being *empowered for service.* I.e., God wants a certain person to be able to perform some work or to carry out some responsibility in a way that will help to fulfill some purpose of God here on earth. This is what we sometimes call "spiritual gifts," or "gifts of the Spirit." The Spirit comes upon that person in order to equip or empower him or her for service in His kingdom.

These gifts can involve miraculous powers (e.g., being able to work miracles, to speak in tongues, to speak inspired messages from God—1 Corinthians 12:28), or they may involve just an enhancement of natural abilities (such as teaching, leadership, or showing mercy—Romans 12:7-8). Also, the Holy Spirit has come upon people for this purpose of empowerment both in Old Testament times and in New Testament times. Many individuals within Old Testament Israel were so empowered, including all the prophets and judges, and including at least some of the kings of Israel. This is where David comes into the picture. When God chose David to replace Saul as king over Israel, the prophet Samuel anointed him with oil, "and the Spirit of the LORD came mightily upon David from that day forward" (1 Samuel 16:13). This is when he received the Holy Spirit.

This empowerment by the Spirit is NOT directly related to salvation. In Old Testament times the Holy Spirit came upon individuals for empowerment for service, but *not for salvation*. When David received the Holy Spirit at the time he was anointed to be king, this did not affect his salvation status. (He probably was already saved at this point.) Not all saved people had the empowerment of the Holy Spirit in Old Testament times, and even someone who was *not* saved could have the Spirit in this sense (e.g., the pagan prophet Balaam, Numbers 24:2).

So what was David praying in Psalms 51:11? We must remember the occasion that prompted this prayerful psalm, namely, David's adulterous episode with Bathsheba (see 2 Samuel 11 & 12). Here in Psalms 51 he is inspired to write about his own heart-felt repentance for this sin. One thing he is concerned about is that God might punish him for this sin by removing him from his position as king over Israel, and even by no longer using him to write inspired songs of praise (i.e., psalms).

David knew that he had received the empowering presence of the Spirit as recorded in 1 Samuel 16:13 (see 2 Samuel 23:2). He also knew that when God rejected Saul as king, "the Spirit of the LORD departed from Saul" (1 Samuel 16:14). Knowing these things, in Psalms 51:11 David prays that God would not do the same thing to him that He had done to Saul. I.e., he prays that God would not withdraw the equipping presence of the Spirit from him, thus effectively ending his service to God. His concern has nothing to do with the saving presence of the Holy Spirit, because this was something no one had or even knew about in Old Testament times.

SECTION TWO: MISCELLANEOUS STUDIES ON
THE HOLY SPIRIT

Now, on the other hand, there IS such a thing as the SAVING presence of the Holy Spirit. In this case, some people have received the Holy Spirit for the purpose of being *empowered for holy living*. This did not begin until the day of Pentecost as recorded in Acts 2; it is one of the great blessings associated with the Messianic age and the Church of Jesus Christ. The individuals who receive this presence of the Spirit are those who obey the gospel (Romans 10:16; 2 Thessalonians 1:8), as announced by the apostle Peter beginning in Acts 2:38-39 (see Acts 5:32).

In this case the Holy Spirit does not "come *upon*" a person to empower him or her for service; rather, the Spirit "comes *into*" a person and indwells his very life and body (Romans 8:9-11; 1 Corinthians 6:19). The immediate result of this indwelling of the Spirit is the beginning of the second aspect of the "double cure" of salvation, which involves the inward change of a convert's very heart. This is the one-time event called "regeneration" (see Titus 3:5), and also being "born again" (see John 3:5).

The ongoing result of this indwelling of the Spirit is the continuation of this second aspect of the double cure, namely, "sanctification." The Spirit continues to dwell within the Christian's life for the purpose of giving him or her the spiritual power to overcome sin (Romans 8:13) and to live a holy and virtuous life (Ephesians 3:16; Philippians 2:13). (See my books on the Holy Spirit for more information on this aspect of the Spirit's work: *The Holy Spirit: A Biblical Study*; and *Power from on High: What the Bible Says About the Holy Spirit*.)

It is impossible to overemphasize the magnitude of the blessing God has bestowed upon us Christians by giving us this indwelling presence of His Holy Spirit. We should indeed pray that God will never withdraw His Spirit from us in this sense, which could happen if we were to truly "fall from grace" and lose our salvation by ceasing to trust in Jesus as our Lord and Savior.

But this is NOT what was going on with David in Psalms 51. He did not even *have* this saving presence of the Spirit in the first place, since this is something that did not begin until the day of Pentecost in Acts 2. He was indeed praying for God's help in being cleansed of his sinful ways, as in verse 10; but he was also praying for God not to cast him aside as prophet and king, as in verse 11. In this latter case he was praying for God not to remove the equipping presence of the Spirit from him, which he had received in 1 Samuel 16:13.

CAN THE HOLY SPIRIT DWELL
WITHIN SINNERS?

QUESTION: How does the Holy Spirit live in us as we sin? Is not the HOLY Spirit the very opposite of sin? How can they BOTH be present in us?

ANSWER: First we will note that the Holy Spirit *does* dwell within Christians. This is one of the new blessings of the Messianic age, beginning on Pentecost in Acts 2:38. The Spirit is given to us in Christian baptism, and continues to dwell within us. "Do you not know that your body is a temple of the Holy Spirit within you, whom you have from God?" (1 Corinthians 6:19). We are told that "the Spirit of him who raised Jesus from the dead dwells in you" (Romans 8:11).

Second, we will also note that *sin* does also dwell within Christians. Let's make sure we have a precise understanding of what happens when we are saved. First, our sins are *forgiven*. This does not mean they are removed; they are *covered* by the blood of Christ (see Romans 4:7-8); and we are justified, or declared righteous. Second, the Holy Spirit comes to dwell within us, and the immediate result is that we are *regenerated* (born again, newly created, raised up from spiritual death). This also does not mean that our sins are removed, nor does it mean that our sin-diseased natures are completely healed. Rather, it means that our sin-riddled spirits are brought back to life, and that the *process* of healing (i.e., sanctification) has begun, and that it will continue throughout our lives.

Here is another thing. Romans 3:23 says that "all have sinned and fall short of the glory of God." "Have sinned" is past tense, but "fall short of the glory of God" is present tense. Even as Christians we are not perfect (not completely healed, as indicated above). Sin is not just in our actions but in our attitudes and states of mind. Can we really say that we are *completely* free from pride, anger, impatience, lust, envy, greed, enmity, and other such sinful states? Do we have *perfect* love, faith, kindness, self-control, and other such virtues? No, we continue to "fall short" of sinless perfection. But the Holy Spirit is still within us!

We may also consider Paul's confession concerning his own indwelling sin. He says that he does not understand his own actions, because he does the very things he hates. "So now it is no longer I who do it, but sin that dwells within me. For I know that nothing good dwells in me, that is, in my flesh" (Romans 7:15-18). He continues, "For I do not do the good I want, but the evil I do not want is what I keep on doing. Now if I do what I do not want, it is no longer I who do it, but sin that dwells within me" (Romans 7:19-20).

Many will say that Paul is not talking here about his present Christian life, but about his pre-Christian life. I disagree with this, and in my commentary on Romans I have explained the many reasons why we must see him as describing his Christian experience. (See *The College Press NIV Commentary on Romans*, first edition, 1996; I:443-445). But how does Paul explain this continuing presence of sin in his life? By distinguishing between the two aspects of his life: his redeemed *spirit*, which is what was regenerated and changed in his baptism (Romans 6:1-6), and his as-yet-unredeemed body—the "body of sin" (Romans 6:6), in which the sin still dwells. On this distinction between the redeemed inner being or mind, and the as-yet unredeemed bodily members, or flesh, or "body of death," see Romans 7:21-25. (I have explained this throughout my commentary on Romans 6 through 8.)

But how can we explain the fact that both of these things are true at the same time? Let's focus on this question: why do we receive the gift of the indwelling Spirit in the first place? What is the purpose of His indwelling? The answer is that the Holy Spirit comes into our lives and very bodies for the purpose of empowering us to fight and conquer the sin that constantly besets us. To think that the Spirit could or would live in us only if we do *not* sin is equivalent to thinking that a doctor will visit us and treat us only if we have no diseases or ailments. When the bank robber Willie Sutton was asked WHY he robbed banks, his reputed reply was, "Because that's where the money is." Why does the Spirit live within us who are sinners? Because that's where the sin is! And His job is to enable us to fight against sin, and to "put to death the deeds of the body" (Romans 8:13). He dwells within our very bodies, which themselves continue to be indwelt by sin. "Thus he is in position to do battle for us in the very place where we need him most" (*Commentary on Romans*, 1st ed., I:470).

QUESTION: Yes, but we have been taught that sin and God cannot inhabit the same space at the same time. How can the Spirit and sin inhabit the same temple?

ANSWER: Yes, we have been taught that, but it is possible that we were taught wrong! Perhaps we should think of another possibility: maybe we should not think of the transcendent God (here, the Holy Spirit) as "inhabiting space," in the same sense that created reality does.

QUESTION: OK, but what might we have been taught wrong?

ANSWER: Just the idea that "sin and God could not inhabit the same space." What we are doing here is confusing metaphysics with ethics. The Spirit is "present" in some metaphysical sense in the life of every

Christian, even though no Christian has a perfectly sin-free heart and thus to some extent is in ethical conflict with the Spirit. This does not drive the Spirit out, but makes his presence even more needed and precious.

It is true that the moral nature of God (including the Holy Spirit) is the opposite of sin. But this simply means that he hates sin, and that he cannot and will not do something that is sinful. It does not mean that he cannot have any CONTACT with sin. As an analogy, a doctor hates cancer, but he treats people whose bodies are riddled with it. Also, a fireman hates fire, but he enters a burning building and risks his life to save people trapped in it.

Remember this: Jesus, though he is God the Son, took the sin of the world upon himself so that he might bear its penalty in our place. Indeed, "God made him who had no sin to be sin for us, so that in him we might become the righteousness of God" (2 Corinthians 5:21, NIV). "He himself bore our sins in his body on the tree" (1 Peter 2:24). His very redemptive mission required Him to be in the most intimate contact with sin for the purpose of destroying its power over us. Likewise with the Holy Spirit: His very salvific purpose for indwelling us requires Him to come face to face with the sin in our lives every day, for the purpose of destroying it (Romans 8:13).

SECTION THREE

STUDIES IN DEMONOLOGY

ALL ABOUT DEMONS: WHO? WHAT? WHEN?

Whenever the subject of demons is mentioned today, a common response is skepticism. Many are skeptical about the very existence of demons. Some deny the existence of anything spiritual or supernatural, whether it be divine or demonic. Many sincere Christians believe in God and accept Jesus as their Savior, but they reject the existence of personal demonic spirits.

How do they explain the Bible's and Christ's references to demons, then? This was merely an accommodation, they say, to the ignorance and superstition of the time. Biblical characters thought to be "demon possessed" were actually suffering from forms of mental illness. Jesus knew this, of course; He was simply going along with the popular notion.

This whole approach to the subject of demons must be rejected. It raises serious questions about the integrity of Jesus, and it undermines the authority of God's Word. It leaves us wondering what *other* "superstitions" Jesus and the Biblical writers might have been accommodating. Besides, there is absolutely no Biblical basis for such a view. We must reject it and unhesitatingly accept the clear Scriptural testimony that demonic spirits do exist.

Skepticism about demons takes another form, though. Many Christians believe they exist, but are skeptical about their present-day activity. A common view is that demons were allowed to invade Palestine during Christ's ministry so that He could demonstrate His lordship over them. But their activity was curtailed after the apostolic age, we are told.

I must admit that for a long time this was my own view. Shortly after I graduated from Bible college, however, I changed my mind. I am convinced that demons are hard at work in many ways today, particularly in the area of the occult. I am also convinced that skepticism and ignorance about demonic activity today pose a threat even to Christians. Thus I am convinced that we need to be made aware of the reality and the nature of the work of demons in our age. This essay is intended to produce such awareness.

I.   WHAT ARE DEMONS?

There is no general agreement as to the identity of demons. In his book *Biblical Demonology* (Scripture Press, 1952), Merrill Unger discusses four major views (pp. 41ff.). Some have thought that demons are the spirits of wicked human beings who have died. Others have suggested that they are the disembodied spirits of a rebellious race of creatures who inhabited the earth prior to Adam and Eve. Still others say that demons might be the monstrous product of mating between angels and women, a view supposedly based on Genesis 6:2.

None of these views has a solid Biblical basis. The most probable explanation of the identity of demons is a fourth view, that they are fallen angels. How can this be?

In addition to the visible universe and no doubt prior to it, God created a whole invisible company of angelic beings who existed in their own created invisible universe (Colossians 1:16). These were by nature pure spirit, and were intended to exist "outside" the sphere of material creation, though they could interact with it. Their number was unimaginably great (see Revelation 5:11; Hebrews 12:22). There were several varieties, including cherubim and seraphim (Exodus 25:20; Ezekiel 1; Isaiah 6:2-6). Apparently there was a hierarchy within their ranks, with some being designated as "chief angels" (i.e., *archangels*, such as Michael).

The purpose of the angelic host was to serve God and carry out His orders. The word "angel" (Greek, *angelos*) means, simply, "messenger."

Many if not most of these angelic creatures have continued faithfully to serve their Creator. At one point, however, there was a fall or a rebellion against God among the angels. The Bible speaks of angels that sinned and whose eternal condemnation is sealed (2 Peter 2:4; see Jude 6).

Who are these angels who sinned? The principal one was undoubtedly Satan, who has been a murderer and a sinner "from the beginning" (John 8:44; 1 John 3:8), i.e., ever since the beginning of our material creation recorded in Genesis 1. When Satan himself was first created he was good and was probably an archangel. We believe this because of Jude 9 and Revelation 12:7, where Satan is paired in combat with the archangel Michael. All the other angels who sinned were probably lower in rank than Satan and have now become his own "angels" or messengers (Matthew 25:41; Revelation 12:7, 9).

These fallen angels who now serve Satan are most probably the demons of which Scripture speaks. The *King James Version* usually translates the Greek word *daimonion* as "devil," but it is better to use the word "devil" only to translate *diabolos*, which refers to Satan alone. (See Revelation 12:9.) Satan is called the ruler or prince of the demons (Matthew 9:34; 12:24). Demons are also called "evil spirits" and "unclean spirits" (e.g., Mark 7:25-30; Luke 7:21).

II. WHAT DO DEMONS DO?

In considering the work of demons, we can assume that their method and goals are the same as Satan's, since they are his angels and simply carry out his orders. So what is Satan trying to do?

Generally, Satan's main goal is to defeat God's plan and purpose in whatever way possible. He tried to ruin this plan at the very beginning by dragging Adam and Eve into sin (Genesis 3). But God had already arranged a solution to this problem, namely, redemption through His Son. When Jesus came, the devil tried to abort this plan by tempting Him to sin (Matthew 4:1-11). Satan did not succeed, though, since Jesus refused to abandon His mission.

What can Satan do now, having failed to block redemption at its fountain? He can only hope to prevent *individuals* from receiving this redemption. Thus each individual is the object of Satan's attack, as the devil "prowls around like a roaring lion, seeking someone to devour" (1 Peter 5:8). Here is where Satan's angels, the demons, enter the picture. Contrary to a popular misconception, Satan is not omnipresent: he cannot be everywhere at the same time. (This is a characteristic possessed only by the Creator; sometimes we forget that Satan is a created being.) Thus he deploys his troops (the demons) throughout the world, and they carry out his work and purposes in his name.

Specifically, how do Satan and his angels hope to accomplish their work? There are three main lines of attack. The first and most important is the Satanic assault upon our *minds* through deceit and false teachings. The devil's main tactic is deception. He is called "the father of lies" (John 8:44) who "deceives the whole world" (Revelation 12:9). He works through disguises (2 Corinthians 11:14), schemes (Ephesians 6:11), and snares (2 Timothy 2:26). He and his demons are explicitly identified as the source of false teaching (1 Timothy 4:1). He is even permitted to accompany his falsehoods with "all power and signs and false wonders" (2 Thessalonians 2:9) to delude the unwary. See also Revelation 16:14; Matthew 7:21-23; 24:24.

Satan's second line of assault is upon our *wills*, through temptation. Cartoons sometimes show a devilish little imp perched upon a sinner's shoulder, whispering into his ear. Though we realize it does not happen in this way, we are not sure just what the mechanics of temptation are. Whatever Satan or his demons do must happen below the level of consciousness. The will is drawn into a sinful decision, which is usually followed by a sinful deed. See John 13:2; 1 John 3:8-10.

Finally, Satan attacks individuals by assaulting their *bodies*. His demons may enter through some unguarded gate of the mind and actually take possession of specific bodily parts or functions (including the processes of the brain). This is called demonization (demon possession or oppression), and can be devastating to the victim's personality and well-being. See Matthew 8:28-33; 17:14-18; Luke 13:10-13.

We must remember that all these types of activity have the same goal: preventing sinners from receiving and keeping God's true salvation.

III. ARE DEMONS ACTIVE TODAY?

The question of present-day demon activity usually calls forth a remarkable display of strong feelings and strong convictions. This is true because most people recognize that a great deal is at stake here. Those who deny demon activity today usually do so because they are convinced that it is inconsistent with certain important Biblical doctrines. Those who affirm it are concerned about the real suffering and loss that occur when the demonic danger is minimized or denied.

Since I believe in the reality of demonic activity today, I share this latter concern. I am concerned for those who are harassed by evil spirits to the point that they suffer physical, emotional, or spiritual pain. I am concerned for the many who are consigned to mental hospitals because their real problem is undiagnosed. I am concerned about those who have been deluded by demonic miracles and have accepted demonic doctrines given by demonic inspiration. I am concerned because the church is not sounding an adequate warning against the real dangers that exist today in this area, and because the church is largely unprepared to help those who are suffering from demonic oppression.

Demons *are* active today, in every aspect of their work. They still spawn false doctrines and provide supernatural powers and wonders to increase the deception. They still tempt us to sin. And they still are able to oppress and even to possess the bodies of the unwary.

A. The Evidence

We must admit that demons are active today, simply because the evidence for it is overwhelming. The abundant testimony of competent eyewitnesses leaves us no other choice. The only sufficient explanation for a virtual mass of related phenomena is that they have been caused by demons. Other explanations have been suggested: fraud, error, psychological abnormalities or powers, mysterious natural forms, harmless but mischievous spirits, and even God. These may explain some or even many of the current happenings, *but they cannot explain all of them.*

For instance, a person's speaking and conversing in an unlearned foreign language has often been observed in pagan contexts or in connection with apparent demon possession. See Kurt Koch's book, *Demonology Past and Present* (Kregel, 1973), p. 144. Edgar Cayce's documented ability to diagnose difficult diseases while in a trance is another example. The demonic origin of Cayce's powers is confirmed by the circumstances and by the anti-Biblical religious teaching that came from the same trance-source. See Gary North, *None Dare Call It Witchcraft* (Arlington House, 1977), chapter 6. Still another example is "Arigo, surgeon of the rusty knife," the Brazilian peasant who performed automatic, painless, instant operations on thousands of his countrymen. His ability came from a spirit that took possession of him, he said. See John G. Fuller, *Arigo, Surgeon of the Rusty Knife* (Crowell, 1974). We could also cite Ouija boards that move under their "own" power, poltergeist ("haunted house") phenomena, visible instant healings by witches and sorcerers, and people who have all the Biblical symptoms of demon possession.

I have talked with many who have been eyewitnesses of such phenomena and who are convinced that only demonic activity can explain them. There are numerous books (besides those mentioned above) that document such cases with all the objectivity and scholarly care that can reasonably be required. Some of these are as follows: Merrill Unger, *Demons in the World Today* (Tyndale House, 1971); Victor Ernest, *I Talked with Demons* (Tyndale House, 1970); Raphael Gasson, *The Challenging Counterfeit* (Logos, 1966); John Nevius, *Demon Possession* (Kregel, 1968); Malachi Martin, *Hostage to the Devil* (Reader's Digest Press, 1976); John Richards, *But Deliver Us from Evil* (Seabury, 1974); and John W. Montgomery, editor, *Demon Possession* (Bethany Fellowship, 1976).

Much of the most convincing testimony comes from missionaries and others who have been intimately associated with pagan, idol-worshiping cultures. One of the very best books from this perspective—indeed, one of the best overall—is Robert Peterson's *Are Demons for Real?* (Moody, 1972). Peterson was a missionary to Borneo for several years, during which he witnessed numerous examples of demon activity. Here is one of them:

> Every Chinese community in this land has its order of priests and sorcerers, each of whom has a duty to perform in the idolatrous ceremonies. From among these priests, some are chosen to perform acts of self-laceration under the influence of evil spirits. The priests sit in specially made chairs, the parts in contact with the body being made out of spikes and knives. I found these knives as sharp as razor blades and could detect no sham in the whole performance. The priest chosen for the ceremony is first prepared by the worship of demons and a deliberate invitation for the demon to possess the body. As the demon enters an immediate change is noticed: the eyes become glazed and the possessed man dances about with such a light step that he seems to have overcome the power of gravity. His words emanate, not from the vocal chords, but from the pit of the stomach and he may issue commands to another attendant priest in a language not his own and even one that he cannot normally speak at all.
>
> When the demon's wishes have been fulfilled (for the demon is now in control), knives, daggers or sharpened bamboo sticks are handed to the man. I have witnessed these instruments being thrust through the cheeks, the tongue, and sometimes through vital organs of the body without a trace of bleeding or feeling of pain. The demon-possessed man jumps about waving a large sword in the air and then,

with a mighty leap, seats himself on the chair on which he is carried about the town as an object of worship ... (p. 16).

B.   Biblical Teaching

Such events would seem to leave no doubt that demonic spirits are working today. Why is it, then, that many still reject this conclusion? Mainly because they believe that certain Biblical teaching rules out any demonic activity past the apostolic age.

Is this the case? Is there any Biblical reason to deny present-day demon activity? If there is, we must yield to it. But I am convinced that no teaching of Scripture limits the work of demons to the apostolic age.

One major objection to continuing demonic activity is based upon the Biblical teaching that Satan was bound through the death and resurrection of Christ at His first coming. That Satan was indeed bound at that time is, I think, the proper understanding of Revelation 20:1-3 and Matthew 12:25-29. To interpret this as eliminating all Satanic and demonic working goes too far, however, since the devil still "prowls around like a roaring lion, seeking someone to devour" (1 Peter 5:8). Our struggle is still "against the rulers, against the powers, against the world forces of this darkness, against the spiritual forces of wickedness" (Ephesians 6:12).

That Satan has been bound means that his power has been limited, and this limitation is specified in Revelation 20:3: "so that he would not deceive the nations any longer." Satan's power to deceive and entrap whole nations has been limited by the spread of the gospel of truth. Anyone who hears and believes and obeys this truth is set free from Satan's power—in every way. Through the power of Christ we *can* escape Satan's grip. But it is not automatic; one must consciously accept the truth and choose to be rescued from the devil. On the other hand, those who ignore or reject the truth subject themselves to every snare of Satan: the traps are still set.

The other major objection to continuing demonic activity, especially in the form of possession or oppression, is based on the Bible's teaching that miraculous spiritual gifts have ceased. The assumption is that the continuation of demon possession would require the continuation of certain miraculous gifts, especially the ability to cast out demons (Mark 16:17) and the gift of discernment (1 Corinthians 12:10).

I agree that miraculous spiritual gifts have ceased, but I do not agree that the discernment and the expulsion of demonic spirits require miraculous powers. Regarding discernment, the people in Jesus's day knew when a demon was present (see Mark 7:25-30). Comparing contemporary cases with Biblical examples gives adequate grounds for identifying a demonic presence. See Kurt Koch, *Demonology*, pp. 136-140, for a summary of the "eight marks of demon possession" found in Luke 8:26-39.

Regarding the expulsion of demons, it is true that miraculous powers were employed in New Testament times to bring about instantaneous deliverance. It is also true that in New Testament times miraculous powers were used to accomplish immediate and complete healing of diseases. But even though *miraculous* healing power is no longer available, we still invoke (through prayer) the supernatural *providential* power of God to heal the sick—which He often applies, according to His higher wisdom and will. In the same way, through prayer and fasting and calling upon God to intervene providentially, the demon-distressed can be delivered today. No miraculous powers are necessary.

(It is important to remember that demons work in many ways besides full-fledged demon *possession*. It is not a choice between this or nothing. There are lesser degrees of intrusion or involvement.)

C. "Be on the Alert!"

Demonic invasion is not an arbitrary, random possibility against which there is no protection. As Christians we remember God's promise: "Greater is He who is in you than he who is in the world" (1 John 4:4). If we consciously trust in the protecting power of Jesus Christ, this "shield of faith" will "extinguish all the flaming arrows of the evil one" (Ephesians 6:16).

Also, it is quite clear that engaging in certain sinful activities is issuing an open invitation to demons to come into one's life. This includes all forms of idolatry, as 1 Corinthians 10:14-21 indicates. Gross, extended immorality may also have the same result. Voluntarily surrendering control of the mind to unknown powers (as through drugs or mysticism) invites demonic invasion. Finally, seeking unusual knowledge or powers through occult activities is an open door through which demons may enter. This is one of the main reasons why God has forbidden such activities, beginning in Deuteronomy 18:9-14. If we will heed God's warnings, we need not fear demonic intrusion.

Those who disregard the warnings and are not trusting in the protecting power of Jesus Christ may find themselves demonically oppressed. (Some, including myself, believe this can happen even to Christians if they stumble in any of these matters.) Deliverance is possible through God's providential power, however. Those who desire further information on this point may find the following books to be useful: Kurt Koch, *Occult Bondage and Deliverance* (Kregel, 1970); Hobart Freeman, *Angels of Light* (Logos, 1969); and Merrill Unger, *What Demons Can Do to Saints* (Moody, 1977). [Writing in 2018, I will add with the highest recommendation Neil T. Anderson's works, especially *The Bondage Breaker* (several editions).]

These books are recommended only for their practical suggestions for helping the demonically oppressed. They contain numerous doctrinal errors which should be discerned.

SPIRITUAL WARFARE AND THE WORD OF GOD

"For our struggle is not against flesh and blood, but against the rulers, against the powers, against the world forces of this darkness, against the spiritual *forces* of wickedness in the heavenly *places*" (Ephesians 6:12).

Carolyn Butler, missionary to Africa, contends that the typical American Christian does not really believe this verse. "Our religious tradition, our humanistic education and scientific mindset, have blinded us to the reality, the actuality, of that spirit world that Paul describes in Ephesians 6. We don't believe there are spiritual forces in heavenly places that are the real enemy," she says. "The spiritual armor has been relegated to flannelgraph boards and Satan has been caricatured right out of our daily thinking" ("Channeling the Grace of God to an Animistic Society," *Hundredfold*, July-Dec. 1991, p. 30).

Butler is right. We need to wake up and heed the words of the Apostle Peter: "Be of sober *spirit*, be on the alert. Your adversary, the devil, prowls around like a roaring lion, seeking someone to devour" (1 Peter 5:8). Every Christian is a personal target of Satan, marked for conquest. Satan is after your soul, and he will get it if he can!

Satan pursues us on three levels. He attacks our MINDS through false teachings, our WILLS through temptation, and our BODIES through demonization. But God has not left us defenseless in this battle.

Our God has given us *His own Word, the Bible,* both as a defense against the devil and as a weapon of attack. How is this so?

I. HOW THE WORD OF GOD PROTECTS US FROM SATAN'S LIES

Ever since his first sin, Satan's main purpose has been to thwart God's purposes for His creation. At the heart of his fallen nature, the devil is a liar. In John 8:44 Jesus declares that the devil "does not stand in the truth because there is no truth in him. Whenever he speaks a lie, he speaks from his own *nature,* for he is a liar and the father of lies." Thus Satan's main tactic or strategy in his war against God is *deception.*

Satan is the one "who deceives the whole world" (Revelation 12:9; see Revelation 20:3, 7-10). He blinds the minds of the unbelieving (2 Corinthians 4:4). He concocts evil plans (2 Corinthians 2:11) and schemes (Ephesians 6:11); he lays snares or traps for us (2 Timothy 2:26). His evil spirits work through false prophets (1 John 4:1-3). Many will fall prey to these "deceitful spirits and doctrines of demons" (1 Timothy 4:1).

In other words, Satan's main tactic is to gain control of the minds and thoughts of human beings. The "doctrines of demons" are everywhere. Consciously or unconsciously, the false doctrines and false beliefs of the world are inspired by the devil and his angels.

Ben Alexander, a converted British spiritualist and dedicated opponent of Satan's wiles, tells the following story.

Once my wife, Miranda, went to a séance before she became a Christian. At this séance ... a spirit had taken control of a female medium's voice and was speaking through the woman in a masculine voice and giving my wife information pertaining to astrology. After the spirit had finished speaking the spirit asked my wife if there were any questions. My wife said, "Yes, how is it you are able to speak through that woman in a completely different voice, a masculine voice".... The spirit entity speaking through the woman in a different voice said to my wife, "Don't be stereotyped. Everybody wants us to take control of their vocal chords. We, in the spirit world, are not so much interested in taking control of your vocal chords as we are in taking control of your thoughts. Then, when we have control of your thoughts we can give our philosophical messages from the spirit world to help you." Suddenly the whole thing fell into focus. The desire of these demons was to take control mainly of our minds. Then when they had control of our minds they literally had control of our bodies, souls, and actions (*Exposing Satan's Power*, VI/2 [April 1978], p. 1).

Satan is a liar! Satan is the author of the false religions of the world. Demons and idols go hand in hand (1 Corinthians 10:14-22; Psalms 106:38; Revelation 9:20). The founders of major cults testify that they were told to do so by voices from the "spirit world." These include Sun Moon, founder of the "Moonies," or Unification Church; Victor Paul Wierwille, founder of The Way International; and Joseph Smith, founder of Mormonism. The heart of the occult (and its high-tech, yuppie form— the New Age Movement) is spiritism, or deliberate attempts to contact the "spirit world."

Satan is a liar! Make no mistake: the false doctrines of the *secular* world are no less demonically inspired than false religious beliefs. Colossians 2:8 warns us not to be taken captive by false philosophies and empty deception. In modern Western history no doctrines of demons have been more successful than evolutionism, communism, materialism, relativism, secular humanism, and postmodernism.

Satan is a liar! Psalms 2:2-3 paints this picture of rebellion against Yahweh and His Christ: "The kings of the earth take their stand and the rulers take counsel together against the LORD and against His Anointed, saying, 'Let us tear their fetters apart and cast away their cords from us!'" The modern versions of these Satanic rebels are the culture-kings: the idols of the entertainment world, those who rule the media, the lords of liberal politics, the dictators of politically-correct science and education, the promoters of the anti-Christian, so-called "social justice" movement.

Satan is a liar! In the religious context, Satan's deception is compounded by his ability to work miracles through his human agents. These are the "power and signs and false wonders" (literally, "wonders of falsehood") of 2 Thessalonians 2:9. This happens even in the context of Christianity. Jesus says that many will sincerely *prophesy* in His name (a term that includes speaking in tongues; see Acts 2:17-18), cast out demons in His name, and perform many miracles in His name. But He will reject them with these words: "I never knew you; depart from Me, you who practice lawlessness" (Matthew 7:21-23).

Satan is a liar! Within the context of the church some of Satan's most subtle and persistent lies have to do with the Bible itself. He causes doubts about the basic doctrines of revelation, inspiration, and inerrancy. He succeeds in causing people to give up their beliefs in other basic Bible teachings, especially those about Jesus Christ and about how to receive salvation. Jesus says that many hear the Word, but "then the devil comes and takes away the word from their heart, so that they will not believe and be saved" (Luke 8:12).

Once Kurt Koch, the famous Evangelical expert on demonology and the occult, was visiting a Bible college in Manila. While he was there one of the students came under severe demonic attack, and Koch was asked to help in a deliverance session. There were fifty demons, and the session lasted nineteen and one-half hours. Koch describes part of the interaction with the demons thus (from his book, *Demonology, Past and Present*, pp. 142ff.):

> In the process of all this, one of the teachers commanded the voices, "In the name of Jesus tell us your name." "Rakrek," the voice replied. "Where do you come from?" the teacher continued. "From Manchuria," came the reply. "In the name of Jesus tell us why you have come to our school!" "You have a good school. We have come to bring in modernism and liberalism. You won't be able to stop us. They are our friends." I thought at the time how good it would have

been if all the modern theologians of the world could have been present to hear these words.

What can Christians do to successfully fight and defeat the world's great deceiver? First, we must accept the fact that we and everyone else are under attack. Scripture makes it clear that false doctrine is not just an inert, impersonal, passive possibility (like quicksand) that we can avoid as long as we do not actively pursue it. No! As an instrument of Satan it is something he throws in our pathway to cause us to stumble; it is something he chases us with to throw over our heads like a net or a lariat. If we are not actively and consciously defending ourselves against "the schemes of the devil" (Ephesians 6:11), then we will surely become his captives.

Second and specifically, we must *know the truth*. In Ephesians 6:11-18 God tells us He has provided us with all the armor and weaponry we need to defend ourselves against our spiritual enemies. When we examine these verses we learn this crucial fact: *knowledge of the truth* is the most basic form of defense against Satan. In verse 14 truth is named as the very first piece of armor to be put on: "having girded your loins with truth." Jesus says, "And you will know the truth, and the truth will make you free" (John 8:32).

The only sure source of truth is "the sword of the Spirit, which is the word of God"—another basic item in our spiritual armory (Ephesians 6:17). Jesus says God's Word is truth, and that this truth is what sets us apart and protects us from the evil one (John 17:15-17). Our "anointing" (of which 1 John 2:20-27 speaks) is the true Word of God itself, which guards us against lies and deceit. God's Word is "a lamp to my feet and a light to my path" (Psalms 119:105). In Biblical imagery "light" stands for truth; "darkness" stands for falsehood. Thus the truth of God's Word enables us to defeat "the world forces of this darkness" (Ephesians 6:12).

When we refer here to "the Word of God," we are of course speaking of the Bible. To be sure, Jesus Himself is the living Word (John 1:1) and the living Truth (John 14:6), but the Bible is His own spoken and written Word of truth (John 16:12-14). Jesus says of this written word, "Scripture cannot be broken" (John 10:35). It is the divinely-forged, unbreakable sword against which all of Satan's lies are shattered.

Since Satan's main tactic is deception, it is no wonder that he spends so much time and energy attacking the Bible, the one sure source of truth. He knows it is the light that exposes the doctrines of his demons and that protects us from his lying schemes and snares.

Thus from our point of view one of the most important aspects of spiritual warfare is to make sure that we as God's people do not lose confidence in the Bible, our "sword of the Spirit." We must not allow it to become tarnished and weakened in our minds. When Satan convinces us that the Bible is not fully inspired and fully inerrant, we have allowed him to neutralize and destroy our main weapon against him. Without an inerrant Bible, we have no sure source of truth, no light to dispel the darkness of Satan's lies.

Our first line of defense against our spiritual enemies, then, is to *know the truth* (John 8:32) as taught in God's Word. Serious, well-informed Bible study is not an option for Christian soldiers; it is our basic training. Trying to stand against Satan without a knowledge of Bible doctrines is like going to battle with no bullets in your gun.

Knowing what the Bible teaches is not enough, however. We must also *believe the truth* (2 Thessalonians 2:12), i.e., accept the Bible as truth. This must be more than just some passive, implicit faith that says, "Sure, I believe whatever the Bible says." We must have an active faith in its teachings, a firm confidence in its ability to protect us against Satanic deception.

But even this is not enough to guard us against the devil's worst attacks. Paul says the only way to avoid the "deception of wickedness" along with those who perish is to *love the truth* (2 Thessalonians 2:10). We must take it into our hearts, and delight in it, and guard it, and wield it boldly and proudly in our personal lives and in our church activities.

II. HOW THE WORD OF GOD PROTECTS US FROM SATAN'S TEMPTATIONS

The general character of Satan can be summed up in one word: he is EVIL. He became this way through his free-will choice to sin (2 Peter 2:4). He is called "the evil one" (e.g., Matthew 13:19, 38; John 17:15). His demonic subordinates are called "evil spirits" (Luke 7:21; 8:2; Acts 19:12-16). He and those who follow him are characterized by lawlessness (2 Thessalonians 2:3-9), which is the essence of sin (1 John 3:4).

Part of Satan's purpose is to make us like himself, so that it could be said of us, "You are of your father the devil, and you want to do the desires of your father" (John 8:44). He wants us to share his sin, and thus share his condemnation (Matthew 25:41).

To this end the devil attacks our *wills*. He puts pressure on us, trying to persuade us to sin against God. He exploits our spiritual weaknesses, and stokes the fires of our sinful desires. We call this *temptation*. Every time we sin, we have lost a skirmish to the devil.

One of our major defenses against temptation is once more the power of the Word of God. The "sword of the Spirit" is useful for defense as well as offense. It helps us intercept and deflect the influence Satan directs against our wills.

Because the Word of God is so important in our battle against Satan, it is no wonder that some of his strongest temptations are focused on how we use the Bible. We can assume that one of his highest priorities is to tempt us to neglect serious Bible study, so that the Word fails to become deeply rooted in our lives. The result is that the Word cannot function as a protection against further temptations to sin. The desire to sin becomes stronger than our love for the Word, warping our wills to the point where we callously ignore it or suppress it or even openly defy it. Then we become like those in the parable, who at first "receive the word with joy" but "have no firm root." Thus "they believe for a while, and in time of temptation fall away" (Luke 8:13).

For those who have developed a deep love for God's Word and who have let its roots sink deep into their lives, Satan's temptations can be more subtle. When direct temptation cannot overcome our commitment to the Law of God, sometimes the devil's ploy is to lead us to seek alternative interpretations of crucial Biblical texts. Through demonic suggestion we are capable of doing what the Apostle Peter warns us against: distorting and twisting Scripture to our own destruction (2 Peter 3:16). Through clever and creative reinterpretations we convince ourselves that what others may think is sin in fact is not.

Examples of this latter problem are feminists who distort the Bible's teaching on gender roles and squeeze it into the mold of egalitarianism; and homosexuals who pervert every Biblical reference to this sin, claiming that none of its condemnations is talking about loving and committed sexual relationships between those who are homosexual "by nature."

The question we must ask is this: how can we use the Word of God most effectively in our battle against temptation? Again, we must *know*, *believe*, and *love* the truth of God's Word. We know that when Jesus was tempted, He quoted Scripture (Matthew 4:1-11). Only an intimate familiarity with the Bible will enable us to do the same. When temptation assails us, by knowing Scripture we can quote a relevant passage and picture ourselves as holding it between us and Satan like a ready sword. At the same time we must believe that God's Word is truly powerful enough to defeat the devil, being confident like Luther that "one little word shall fell him." We must remember the imagery of Revelation 19:15, where Jesus is pictured as victoriously confronting His foes with a sharp sword coming out of His mouth. (See John MacArthur, Jr., *How to Meet the Enemy* [Victor, 1992], pp. 148-149.)

It is indeed important to know and believe the truth, but something more is necessary to ward off temptation. These are exercises of the intellect, but temptation is an onslaught against the will. We can strengthen our wills to resist temptation only when we have developed a deep *love* for the truth (2 Thessalonians 2:10). Loving the truth is really no different from loving God Himself. To love God "with all your mind" (Matthew 22:37) means to love His Word and hold it dear, and to want to honor Him by obeying it not just outwardly but from your heart (Romans 6:17). To love God's truth means to passionately embrace it, and to bind it to your very life and self. It means to make it such a vital and inseparable part of your very own being that you would rather die than go against it, that you would rather pluck out your eyes or cut off your hands than to use them to disobey God's Word (Matthew 5:29-30).

We can cultivate our love for God's Word by reading it and studying it, not just as an academic duty but as a devotional exercise. Both are important, but we must remember that these are two different things. All Scripture can be read devotionally, but some parts, such as the Gospels and the Psalms, lend themselves to this purpose more readily than others. Especially useful is a frequent reading of Psalms 119, which dwells on the Psalmist's deep love for God's law. See especially verses 1-5, 20, 35, 40, 44, 47, 72, 97, 103-104, 111-112, 127, 131.

Loving God's Word is a protection against temptation because it is impossible to really love the Word without at the same time hating evil (Romans 12:9). Because he loved God's law, said the Psalmist, he hated every false way and everyone who did not keep His Word (Psalms 119:104, 128, 158). "I hate and despise falsehood, but I love Your law" (Psalms 119:163).

Hating evil comes not only from knowing and meditating upon the laws and commandments of God's Word, but also from knowing and embracing its gospel message. When we know that Christ died for our sins, and when we really understand what that means—that He actually suffered the equivalent of eternity in hell, that He actually took upon Himself the penalty that we deserve because of our sins—if this does not make us hate our sins, nothing will. There is truly *power* in the blood of the Lamb: not just power to take away the guilt and penalty of our sin, but power to take away our *love* for sin and to replace it with a hatred for sin that will repel temptation before it gets close enough to entice us.

III. HOW THE WORD OF GOD PROTECTS US FROM DEMONIZATION

Satan and his demons attack our minds, our wills, and our *bodies*. We know from Scripture that demons can invade, inhabit, and even possess a person's body. This results in varying degrees of demonic control over the body. The general term for such a demonic presence in the body is *demonization*; the term *possession* is reserved for only the most severe cases.

Does demonization occur today, even in America? In my judgment, yes. Can Christians themselves be demonized? Again in my judgment, yes. I know this is controversial, but the evidence for these conclusions is overwhelming. Demonization is a real danger that must be warned against and dealt with.

Two questions must be addressed. First, how can we guard against demonic invasion? Second, how can a person be delivered from demonic presence? The Word of God has an important role in both tasks.

Regarding the first question, demons cannot arbitrarily at their own will invade anyone's body. They must in a sense be invited in, or be given some kind of ground or opportunity for entering. This is an implication of Ephesians 4:27, "Do not give the devil an opportunity." What can give demons an opportunity to invade our bodies? The very things we have discussed under the first two points above: accepting falsehood and yielding to temptation.

On the one hand, opening our minds to accept Satan's lies can be an occasion for demonization. Ernest Rockstad, a pioneer in modern deliverance ministry, says, "One of the most common forms of ground is the believing of lies given the victim by wicked spirits." This is especially true of Satanic lies about God. Accepting the validity of false religions and false spiritual practices is an open door to demonization. Idolaters—those who worship false gods—are very vulnerable. Those who pursue the false gods and false gospels of occultism and the New Age Movement are likewise vulnerable.

Though many Christians refuse to believe it, those who seek modern-day miraculous gifts from the Holy Spirit are often invaded by demonic spirits instead. When tested as to their origin, the "tongues" being spoken by Pentecostals and Charismatics today prove overwhelmingly to be demonic in origin. For example, Kurt Koch wrote that in his judgment "maybe over 95%" of tongues today are from demons (*The Strife of Tongues*, Kregel 1971, p. 35). He later said this estimate is too low, with 99% being more accurate (cited in Grayson Ensign and Edward Howe, *Counseling and Demonization* [Recovery 1989], p. 295). Ensign and Howe say their tests discovered no genuine gift of tongues (ibid., p. 297). Most who actually do this sort of testing find the percentage of demon-inspired tongues to be very great, usually between 90% and 100%. George Birch says, "Our own experience to date has been that out of 207 spirits of tongues tested, all but three have been clearly proven to be demonic. Those three were not clear and neither proved to be of the Holy Spirit" (*The Deliverance Ministry* [Horizon House 1988], pp. 149-150).

How can we protect ourselves against demonic invasion? By a total commitment to the truth of God's Word. We must worship the one true God and accept the one true gospel as taught in the Bible. It is especially important to believe the gospel of the death and resurrection of Jesus with all our hearts. Demons hate and fear the blood of Christ; those who consciously and consistently claim its protection will be safe.

On the other hand, yielding to temptation and indulging in sin and immorality can also be an occasion for demonization. Those in the deliverance ministry testify that some of the most common grounds for demonic invasion are sins such as fornication, adultery, homosexualism, drunkenness, and doing drugs. To persistently indulge in such sins is to open up a crack in your spiritual armor, which demons are always ready to exploit. The best defense against this, of course is to rely on the power of God's Word and God's Spirit to enable us to resist temptation.

The second main question is how a demonized person can be set free from the demons that inhabit his body. Here again the power of the Word of God is a major factor. In this essay I cannot go into every detail concerning the methodology for deliverance from demons; for that I heartily recommend the works of Neil T. Anderson, especially *The Bondage Breaker*. What I will emphasize here is the role of the Word in a successful deliverance.

It is significant that one of the symptoms of demonization is an uncontrollable aversion to all divine things, including the Bible. Kurt Koch calls this "the phenomenon of resistance, an opposition to the things of God" (*Demonology Past and Present*, Kregel 1973, p. 138). For example, a man with occult powers suspected of being demonized reported that "if he wants to read the Bible he gets spots before the eyes. If he hears a person preaching the Word of God he cannot concentrate at all, however hard he tries" (ibid., p. 66). Conrad Murrell calls this symptom "confusion in the mind," with an "inability to think straight especially in respect to the Bible and truth" (*Practical Demonology*, 3 ed., Saber 1982, p. 79). He tells of a demonized young woman who "was unable to pray or to concentrate on Bible study. During the services in which I was preaching it was impossible for her to understand the word" (ibid., p. 68). One specific work of demons, as they themselves report under forced questioning, is "to keep [the demonized person] from studying the Word of God," and "to deceive him ... not to understand the Scripture fully" (Birch, *Deliverance Ministry*, p. 49; see p. 118).

Because the Word of God has power against Satan, it is crucial that those participating in deliverance be fully reliant upon that Word, both as defensive armor and as an offensive weapon. The victimized person must be firmly surrendered to Christ and His Word. The minister or counsellor must have strong faith in the power and the promises of the Word.

In the deliverance session itself, reading and quoting the Bible—wielding the sword of the Spirit—is crucial. Ensign and Howe report thus on their experiences in counseling sessions:

> The demons hate the Word of God, so it is used extensively. In the opening of the session the Scriptures are read, and usually one

person will continue quietly to read Scriptures during the session. Demons can hear the Word even when it is being quietly read at some distance, and often they are brought into manifestation by such reading. They may cover the ears of the person invaded or shout out, "Shut up, I don't want to hear that." Demons have been brought out of hiding and into manifestation by holding the Bible near the invaded person as it is read. This often has infuriated the demon so that he came into manifestation (took control of the person) and tried to tear the Bible apart. In several cases demons did succeed in ripping Bibles apart, using the body of the demonized person to do so (*Counseling and Demonization*, p. 163).

Specific Scripture passages useful for these purposes are given as Psalms 1, 32, 38, 91, 103, Isaiah 41:9-13; Matthew 6:9-13; Mark 5:1-13; Ephesians 1:18-22; 6:10-18; Philippians 2:5-11; Revelation 12:7-12; 19:11-16; 20:1-10. (Ibid., p. 168.)

Ensign has said elsewhere that "evil spirits hate the word, and it stirs them into action." They cannot stand it; they want to oppose it and at the same time flee from it. Ensign and Howe declare that the sword of the Spirit "is a very great part of the armor that God uses in overcoming the resistance of evil spirits" (ibid., p. 163). To drive out an invading demon "we bombard him with Scriptures," they say (ibid., p. 196).

CONCLUSION

We are at war: be not deceived. But we are on the Victor's side: be not afraid. To be safe and victorious, heed these commands of Ephesians 6: "Be strong in the Lord" (v. 10). "Put on the full armor of God" (v. 11). "Stand firm" (v. 14). "Be on the alert" (v. 18). Rest in God's promise in James 4:7, "Resist the devil and he will flee from you."

The decisive battle in spiritual warfare has already been fought—and won—by Jesus Christ (Revelation 12:7-9; 20:1-3; Colossians 2:15). He has left us with every necessary resource for sharing this victory with Him, including His powerful Word.

CAN CHRISTIANS BECOME DEMONIZED?

INTRODUCTION

Most Bible-believers agree that demons are real, and that they are able to enter into and take control of the bodies of individual men and women. Most will agree that such demonized people can be delivered from that demonic presence. However, sincere Christians disagree as to whether demons can enter into or be present in the bodies of Christians. After examining the evidence for this possibility, I have come to the conclusion that Christians can indeed become demonized. As Christian workers we need to be aware of this possibility, and we need to know how to help those who have become so.

I.   THE TESTIMONY OF DELIVERANCE WORKERS

Usually, those who deny that Christians can be demonized (what used to be called "demon-possessed") have had little or no experience in working with demonized people. Their denial is based mainly on how they understand certain Biblical teachings. However, I have noted that those who have had considerable experience in working with the demonized, especially those involved in the ministry of deliverance, are in almost total agreement that true Christian believers are vulnerable to demonization.

My first contact with anyone involved in deliverance ministry was with Brother Grayson Ensign, who had a long history of service as one of our preachers and Bible college professors. When he was teaching at The

Cincinnati Bible Seminary in the 1970s he and associates, including Edward Howe, started Christ's Church Cincinnati in a depressed area of the city. They began to encounter many people who they learned were demonized, and through research and experience became experts in the field of spiritual warfare. In 1984 Ensign and Howe published a book called *Bothered? Bewildered? Bewitched?* It was later revised as *Counseling and Demonization* (Amarillo: Recovery Publications, 1989). I had many discussions with Brother Ensign about what he had learned about demons from his many years of personal experience.

Over the years Brother Ensign helped deliver many hundreds of people from the presence of demons—*all Christians.* His conviction was that a demonized person cannot be truly delivered unless he or she IS a Christian. In a printed classroom lecture titled "Christians and Demons and Christ's Victory," Brother Ensign described several cases in which Christians were delivered from demons, and then said:

> These are just a few of the many soul-shaking testimonies that I could give you of the condition of many of our brothers and sisters and of many preachers. The terrible defeat, apostasy, and tragic ruin in thousands of lives is heartrending and all so needless. In the light of our experience in the past ten years I am as certain as anything that these Christians have been severely harassed by demons, and some of these evil spirits have become internalized. They have invaded the bodies of these Christians and have controlled some part of their bodies, personalities, souls, or minds. It is the deepest conviction of my spirit and the conclusion of the careful research of a number of highly credible brethren that this is the truth before the eternal God. We believe that every child of God could be greatly blessed by going through the procedure of James 5:14ff. Perhaps fifty per cent of church members are in need of liberation from the oppression of evil spirits. The number may be higher than that (p. 4).

In this lecture one of Ensign's main points is this: "THE GREATEST MYTH AND DEADLIEST DECEPTION OF THE DEVIL—A CHRISTIAN CANNOT HAVE A DEMON WITHIN" (p. 11).

The testimony of the Evangelical scholar Merrill F. Unger is just as convincing, though he came to his conclusion in a very different way. In his 1952 book, *Biblical Demonology* (fifth ed., 1963), Unger said: "To demon possession only unbelievers are exposed; to demon influence, both believers and unbelievers. In the one case, the personality is actually invaded, the body inhabited, and a dominating control is gained; while in the other instance, attack is made from without, through pressure, suggestion, and temptation." The saved person "is not liable to demon inhabitation" (1967 printing, p. 100).

Then in his 1971 book, *Demons in the World Today*, Unger admits that "in lands where demon-energized idolatry has flourished unchecked by the gospel for ages, new believers who were delivered from demon possession have been known to become repossessed when they return to their idols." However, "such cases are rarely seen, if ever, in the United States." He grants that his conclusion in *Biblical Demonology* "was inferred, since Scripture does not clearly settle the question. It was based on the assumption that an evil spirit could not indwell the redeemed body together with the Holy Spirit" (116-117). Why did he adjust his view? After the 1952 book was published, Unger got "many letters from missionaries all over the world who question the theory that true believers cannot become demon-possessed." The missionaries had witnessed this phenomenon first-hand. "The claims of these missionaries appear valid," says Unger (117).

Finally, in his 1977 book, *What Demons Can Do to Saints* (Moody, 1977), he goes all the way in the other direction, saying that those who deny satanic power in the life of the regenerated "live in a sort of fool's paradise, imagining that becoming Christians magically shields them from satanic attack or demonic invasion." Even those who grant such influence, but limit it to external attacks [his own former position], do not go far enough. He says, "In cases of serious, persistent, scandalous sin, such as gross immorality or participation in occultism or occult religionism, demons may exercise control over the believer for a time until his sin is confessed and forsaken and deliverance from the evil powers is gained" (55).

Unger adds, "The demon enters, it is true, as a squatter and not as an owner or a guest or as one who has a right there. He comes in as an intruder and as an invader and enemy. But come he does if the door is opened by serious and protracted sin" (60). He continues,

> The Scriptures nowhere plainly state that a true believer cannot be invaded by Satan or his demons. Of course, doctrine must always have precedence over experience. Nor can experience ever furnish a basis for biblical interpretation. Yet, if consistent experiences clash with an interpretation, the only inference possible is that there is something wrong with either the experience itself or the interpretation of the Scripture that runs counter to it. Certainly the inspired Word of God never contradicts valid experience. The sincere truth seeker must be prepared to revamp his interpretation to bring it into conformity with facts as they are (69).

Unger admits that "this is exactly what I have been compelled to do" regarding this question. He has had to reverse the view that he took in the 1952 book (69-70). This book is the result.

Another example is C. Fred Dickason, who has written several excellent books on this subject, including *Angels: Elect and Evil* (Moody, 1975). In 1987 he published another book called *Demon Possession and the Christian*, also published by Moody. In this book he defends the view that Christians can be demonized. The story I heard was that the Moody publishers got so many complaints about Dickason's view on this subject that they decided to drop it. In 1989 it began to be distributed by Good News Publishers.

Another book that I recommend on this subject is Ed Murphy's *The Handbook for Spiritual Warfare* (Thomas Nelson, 1992; revised ed., 2003). On this subject, he says, "The possible demonization of true Christians is the single most controversial area of spiritual warfare today." Yet, "Scripture, church history, and contemporary experience show that under unusual conditions of sin, either their own or the sin of others against them, some believers become demonized" (429). He says,

> Most Christians would categorically reject the possibility of the demonization of true believers. This was my position during most of my years in Christian ministry. In fact most of us who have reversed our position on this matter were brought up with this traditional view of the non-demonization of believers. We changed primarily because of accumulated experience in counseling the demonized (ibid.).

Murphy continues, "My position is that true believers can be demonized. Such demonization can range from mild to severe. I am not affirming that true believers can be demon possessed. They cannot be. Satan does not truly possess anything but his own kingdom of fallen spirits." Rather, "I am affirming that under rare and unusual conditions of sin ... some believers become demonized. Areas of their life can—not necessarily will—come under the direct influence of Satan through demons operating from outside and inside the believer's life" (429-430).

Here is another testimony, this one from George A. Birch in *The Deliverance Ministry* (Horizon House, 1988). He says, "My wife and I believe without a shadow of a doubt that Christians can have demons indwelling them and tormenting them in various areas of their lives. We believe this both from our study of Scripture and from our experience with hundreds of counselees whom we have seen our Lord Jesus Christ deliver from demon invasion over a period of more than 20 years" (89).

The next citation comes from my favorite author on deliverance ministry, Neil T. Anderson. In his excellent book, *The Bondage Breaker* (Harvest House: originally 1993; updated ed., 2000), he says,

Some evangelicals believe that Christians cannot be affected or influenced by demons. Even the suggestion that demonic influence can be part of the problem prompts the hasty disclaimer, "Impossible! I'm a Christian!" Such thinking removes the church from the position of having an adequate answer and helping those who are under attack, and it leaves such people without hope, because we are the only ones who can help them.

Nothing has done greater damage to diagnosing spiritual problems than this untruth. If Satan can't touch the church, why are we instructed to put on the armor of God, to resist the devil, to stand firm, and to be alert? If we aren't susceptible to being wounded or trapped by Satan, why does Paul describe our relationship to the powers of darkness as a wrestling match? Those who deny the enemy's potential for destruction are the most vulnerable to it (p. 22; see p. 114).

It is my estimation that only about 15 percent of the evangelical Christian community is living a free and productive life in Christ (p. 120).

Finally I will cite this statement from Evangelical scholar Clinton E. Arnold, *3 Crucial Questions About Spiritual Warfare* (Baker, 1997). "The biblical, theological, and historical evidence suggests that Christians can be profoundly influenced by evil spirits—even to the extent that it can be said that they are inhabited and controlled by demons" (88).

II.   REASONS WHY SOME DENY THESE CLAIMS

Why do many Christians deny that the demonization of Christians is possible, contrary to such strong testimony to its reality? The main objection is the assumption that a demonic spirit and the Holy Spirit cannot both be present in a person's body at the same time.

This view is common in Christendom, especially in the Restoration Movement. Ben Alexander is an example. He asks, "Can Christians be demon possessed?" He continues, "I have heard this question asked many times in my lifetime.... The answer is quite straightforward, NO! A Christian cannot be demon possessed .... When a Christian receives Christ as their personal Lord and Saviour, the Holy Spirit enters that Christian's body, soul and spirit. God has claimed that person for His own and as a result, demons cannot occupy the same place as the Holy Spirit. Satan knows this and that is why he tries so hard to get people first and have his demons or demonic influence control or affect that person" (*Exposing Satan's Power*, Nov.-Dec. 1994, p. 1).

Joe Beam, from the churches of Christ, in his book, *Seeing the Unseen: A Handbook for Spiritual Warfare* (Howard Publishing Co., 1994), says, "Since a demon has to take control of a person to possess him, one certainly couldn't have possessed [anyone] as long as the Holy Spirit lives in him." This protection is available to all (p. 108). In his publication, *The Witness* (June 2000), Curtis Dickinson says, "The promise by Peter was, 'Repent and be baptized…and you shall receive the gift of the Holy Spirit.' (Acts 2:38) God's spirit dwells in the truly converted, leaving no access for demons" (p. 2).

We should note that this objection is not specifically stated anywhere in the Bible. It is only an inference from the fact of the Holy Spirit's dwelling within us. As we noted above, Merrill Unger acknowledges that his original denial that Christians can be demonized "was inferred, since Scripture does not clearly settle the question. It was based on the assumption that an evil spirit could not indwell the redeemed body together with the Holy Spirit" (*Demons in the World Today*, 116-117). As he acknowledges here, his original conclusion was an inference and an assumption—one that turned out to be inconsistent with actual reality.

As Ed Murphy rightly says, "Those who reject the possible demonization of Christians affirm that the Holy Spirit cannot dwell in the same body with demons. This is a theological presupposition, not a biblical certainty based on scriptural exegesis. Not a single verse of Scripture states that the Holy Spirit cannot or will not dwell in a human body or any other area, where demons are present" (430).

We could ask, what might be the supposed basis for such an inference? Is the objection a metaphysical one or an ethical one? I.e., is it based on metaphysics or on ethics? In terms of metaphysics, is there somehow *not enough room* for both a demonic spirit and the Holy Spirit in the same body? Does the Holy Spirit so fill the believer's life and body that demons are crowded out? Is it simply a matter of power, a question of who is stronger and thus able to drive the other out? Does the Holy Spirit simply issue a divine fiat: "I'm here now; you have to leave"?

Or is it a kind of ethical conflict, the inherent contradiction between good and evil? Is the idea that the HOLY Spirit cannot co-exist with an EVIL spirit?

Regarding the metaphysical problem, it seems to be assumed that if a Christian were demonized, then two spirits would be competing for the same space, in which case the Holy Spirit would always have the advantage (1 John 4:4). I.e., demonic spirits simply cannot compete with the Holy Spirit. In reply, we avow that this whole scenario is misleading. The Holy Spirit and demonic spirits are two completely different kinds of spirit: one is created; the other is uncreated. They can both indwell the same body because they are not doing so in the same sense. Angelic spirits (including demons) are *spatially* present in specific spaces within our universe because of their very nature as created beings. But when the uncreated Holy Spirit is dwelling within a Christian's body, He is "present" on a totally different metaphysical level. The two spirits can be present in the same body because they do not *compete* for the same space, and this is true because they are not present *in the same way*. (As an analogy, consider that both light and water can "occupy" the same space, because they are two kinds of reality and are thus "present" in different ways.)

We are simply saying that the Holy Spirit is divine, infinite, uncreated Spirit; while demonic spirits are finite, created spirits. They are not on the same metaphysical level. Thus they are not "present" in the same way in a person's body. Because they are present on different metaphysical levels, they neither compete nor conflict with one another. The greater metaphysical similarity, and therefore the real conflict and competition, is between a demonic spirit and a person's own spirit. Both are created and finite, and the real struggle is which one will have control of the body. However, in ordinary indwelling the Holy Spirit simply does not indwell the Christian's body in this sense. He may enter a body on this level for specific purposes, such as inspiration or tongues-speaking, but this is a totally different kind of thing and is not limited to Christians.

Regarding the ethical problem, the objection seems to be that a demon is an EVIL spirit, while the Holy Spirit is HOLY. Surely the *Holy* God and an *evil* spirit cannot coexist in the same place. In reply, everything we said in the previous point is relevant here: the two spirits are not present in the same sense and are not "touching" and thus repelling one another like two similar magnetic poles do.

In addition to this, we should also remember that the Holy Spirit is present in the Christian's body at the same time that SIN is still present to some degree in the Christian's life and body. The Holy Spirit does not leave every time a Christian sins. To deny demonization on this grounds, says Murphy, would be similar to this argument: Every Christian is indwelt by the Holy Spirit; the Holy Spirit cannot dwell with sin; therefore Christians cannot sin (431). Such, of course, is not the case. Arnold adds this thought: "If the power of sin can inhabit a Christian's body and exert such a significant influence that Paul could say it 'reigns' (Romans 6:12-13), why do we suppose that another form of evil influence cannot dwell there?" (*3 Questions*, 82).

Another objection is that if a person has a demon, then he must have done something sinful to acquire that demon, thus he would not be in a state of grace anyway. This is a fallacy, though, for two reasons. First, it is not necessarily true that a person must do something sinful to acquire a demon. Sometimes demons are acquired in childhood through no fault of the child, e.g., through the "Law of Generations" or through child abuse.

Evil spirits acquired in such ways do not automatically depart when a person becomes a Christian. (See Murphy, p. 432.)

In the second place, even if a Christian has committed some kind of sin that has given a demon grounds for entry into his life, this sin may not necessarily have resulted in a fall from grace. Assuming that every sin necessarily separates one from the grace of God is a faulty understanding of grace and of what it means to be justified by faith in the blood of Jesus. The fact is that the presence of a demonic spirit does not necessarily imply that a person is lost or outside the grace of God. What is at stake in demonization, at least in the beginning, is one's *sanctification*, but not necessarily his justification.

A final objection has to do with *ownership*. A Christian by definition belongs to Jesus Christ. It is thus impossible for a Christian to be *possessed* by Jesus and *possessed* by demons at the same time. In reply, we say simply that this is just a semantic problem, arising out of the unfortunate terminology, "demon *possession*." The Greek word for this state is *daimonizomai*, which in itself has no connotation of ownership or possession. It means simply "to have a demon, to be demonized." (See Arnold, *3 Questions*, 78-81; Dickason, *Demon Possession*, 37-40.) Other terms that may be used include "invaded by demons," "inhabited by demons," "afflicted by demons," or "demonic presence."

We should note, too, that even a Christian—one who belongs to Jesus—can fail to yield *every aspect* of his life to the control of Christ, and can give demons a ground for being present through that particular aspect (Ephesians 4:27). Consider this statement by Neil Anderson in *The Bondage Breaker*:

> Even though we are secure in Christ and have all the protective armor we need, we are still vulnerable to Satan's accusations, temptations, and deceptions .... Therefore, it is probable that every believer will be influenced by the god of this world. He can gain some measure of control over our lives if we are deceived and believe his lies....

Ownership is never at stake, however. We belong to God, and Satan can't touch who we are in Christ. We may be demon-oppressed, but we are always "Holy-Spirit possessed." But as long as we are living in these natural bodies in this fallen world, we are the target for Satan's fiery darts (114).

Warning: watch out for "once saved, always saved" in Anderson's book!

III. EXAMPLES OF DEMONIZED BELIEVERS IN THE BIBLE?

We might ask if there are any clear examples of demonized believers in the Bible. The answer seems to be negative. Most of the passages warning Christians of Satan's influence do not really say anything about demonization as such. (See Dickason, *Demon Possession and the Christian*, ch. 7.) Some think King Saul is an example (Unger, 99-100; Dickason, 121-123), but they are assuming that a believer cannot fall from grace. (Simon the magician in Acts 8 is in this category; see Dickason, 114-115.)

It is only an inference, but it seems reasonable to assume that at least some of the many pre-Pentecost Jews who were delivered from evil spirits were already believers. Some were "regular synagogue attenders," as in Mark 1:21-28, 39 (Murphy, 432). See Matthew 8:16; Luke 8:1-3. The clearest example is the woman bent double, Luke 13:10-17. Jesus calls her a daughter of Abraham (v. 16), but she had a demon. (See Murphy, 432; Dickason, 123-125; Unger, *WDCDTS*, 100-101.)

The examples given above may not be directly applicable, though, since there was no actual indwelling of the Holy Spirit until the day of Pentecost. This is why Clinton Arnold's suggestion that those whom the evil spirits left in Acts 19:11-12 include Christian believers (*3 Questions*, 91) may be important.

The most important point, though, is the very fact that the Bible *warns* Christians—-yes, *Christians!*—to be on guard against Satan. Such warnings are important because they imply the danger of demonic attack, and may include the possibility of demonic invasion, though this is an inference. Here is a list of such warnings: Ephesians 6:10-18; 2 Corinthians 2:10-11; 10:3-5; 11:3-4; 1 Timothy 4:1; 1 Peter 5:8; Revelation 12:10.

The passage from which this inference may most likely be drawn, though, is Ephesians 4:27: "Do not give the devil an opportunity" (NASB), or "Do not give the devil a foothold" (NIV), or "Nor give place to the devil" (NKJV). On this passage see Murphy, 432; Dickason, 107-8; and especially Arnold, 82, 88. The key word is *topos*, "opportunity, foothold, place." Arnold says, "The one passage in the Epistles that comes closest to the language of demonization is Ephesians 4:26-27 .... The most natural way to interpret the use of *topos* in Ephesians 4:27 is the idea of inhabitable space. Paul is thus calling these believers to vigilance and moral purity so that they do not relinquish a base of operations to demonic spirits" (88).

DELIVERANCE FROM INDWELLING DEMONS

INTRODUCTION

Second Peter 2:4 tells us that some of the angels God originally created as inhabitants of the invisible universe (Colossians 1:16) sinned, and we conclude from other Biblical data that the chief fallen angel (who was probably an archangel) is the one we know now as Satan. We also conclude that demons (evil, unclean spirits) are the lesser fallen angels, and that they now serve Satan's purpose—which is to thwart God's purpose to gather to Himself a family of redeemed human beings whom He can bless with His presence forever.

One aspect of God the Son's incarnation as Jesus Christ was to confront and defeat Satan, which includes disarming him and his armies (Colossians 2:15) and rescuing everyone who has somehow come under Satan's power. "Release to the captives" is part of the gospel mission of Christ (Luke 4:18). He came to bind the strong man and plunder his house, which includes delivering the demonized from indwelling evil spirits (Matthew 12:28-29).

Many years ago I was invited to speak to an annual gathering of many of our Restoration Movement missionaries in Brazil. I knew that Satan has a strong hold on the culture in Brazil, where one of the three main religious forces is animistic spiritism, in which the "spirits" are actually demons. One of the other religious forces there is Pentecostalism, in which demonic spirits are rampantly active under the camouflage of miraculous powers. I also knew that many of our own missionaries had already been seduced into incorporating these "wonders of falsehood" (2 Thessalonians 2:9) into our own churches. Therefore one of my main purposes in speaking to this group was to emphasize the following:

- Demonization is real and is a part of the everyday lives of the people in countries like Brazil.

- The demonization of Christians is often very real. This is important because Pentecostal and Charismatic churches proliferate in animistic societies such as Brazil, and it is necessary to understand that the miraculous manifestations even among the most faithful in these groups most likely are demonic in origin. Otherwise it is a great temptation to accept the validity of this form of Christianity as a presupposition for effective evangelism.

- Deliverance is possible without miraculous power. This is especially important, because the missionaries see a tremendous need to confront the evil spirits and to challenge their power over people. But because most of them have the mistaken belief that the only way to do this is via miraculous power, many of the missionaries themselves have become charismatic.

One might think that the most natural means of deliverance from demonic spirits is conversion, or baptism. The fact is that in the early Christian centuries all pagans were assumed to be demonized, and baptism was usually accompanied by a renunciation of Satan and by an overt exorcism commonly understood to bring deliverance. (One may see Hippolytus's *Apostolic Tradition,* ¶20-21, from the early third century, for details.) Even today some, such as Ben Alexander, consider the act of baptism, in which the indwelling of the Holy Spirit is received, to be an automatic expulsion of any demons that might be present.

Baptism may indeed be the most natural means of such deliverance, but it is not automatic. Unless there is a sincere renunciation of Satan and of all specific conditions and sins that are possible grounds for demonization, the demons still have grounds for remaining, in spite of the baptismal transition to a saved state. Contrary to popular opinion, demons can be present within the bodies of Christians. Some may be carried over from a pre-Christian state; and some may enter afterwards if the Christian participates in demon-friendly activities, even "innocently."

Thus it is important for Christian leaders to have some knowledge of a proper process for delivering such oppressed believers from demonic presence. An awareness of this need, and some methods for confronting it, have been introduced on the Evangelical scene during my lifetime. An early pioneer in this was Ernest Rockstad (1911-1986), who learned to confront and dispel demons mostly by experimentation and experience. Many learned from his writings, including Restoration Movement pioneers, Grayson Ensign and Ed Howe.

The early method of "casting out demons," used by Ensign and Howe in the 1970s and 1980s, was the "power encounter" method. Their book on the subject was first entitled *Bothered? Bewildered? Bewitched? Your Guide to Practical Supernatural Healing* (Recovery Publications, 1984); the second edition was *Counseling and Demonization: The Missing Link* (1988). This method involved a direct confrontation and verbal exchange between the counselor and the demon(s), the counselor usually talking to one of the demons at a time. The purpose was to gain power over a demon by learning its name and its grounds for gaining entry into the person (a la Ephesians 4:27); another purpose was to expose the presence of any other demons that might be hiding within, and to learn which was the one in charge. The ultimate step was to command the demon(s), in the name of Christ, to leave. This method proved to be very successful; Brother Ensign told me at one point in his deliverance ministry that he had already helped to set over 300 Christians free from demons. Not many chose to follow his example, though; this encounter method is actually very intimidating to all involved. (I should note that it does not require miraculous powers.)

Most today agree that the "truth encounter" method (see John 8:32) is better for many reasons. This method does not use direct confrontation with the demonic spirit(s); it relies mainly on sincere surrender to the Lordship of Christ, complete renunciation of all possible grounds for demonic presence, and earnest prayer by and for the demonized person. It does not require miraculous powers, and any mature Christian can be the intercessor for such deliverance. One may follow the instructions set forth in Neil T. Anderson's ground-breaking book, *The Bondage Breaker* (Harvest House). This book came out in 1990, with a new edition in 2000 (the one cited most often here). The one advertised online now is dated 2006, but the page numbers of its table of contents are the same as the 2000 edition, which I am using. Anderson has a great number of other books that are variations and helps centered around this same title.

On pp. 253ff. of his main book, Anderson gives his reasons for using the "truth encounter" method rather than the "power encounter" method.

In what follows here, I will include some material from Grayson Ensign and others, especially when describing the preparation for helping a demonized person. The main material, though, is based on Anderson's work. Whenever anyone asks me what I recommend in this area, I always send them to Anderson.

I. PREPARATION BY THE GUIDE OR COUNSELOR

Here are the recommendations to be followed by the person conducting the deliverance session, i.e., the minister, elder, or counselor. These points are gathered from both Ensign and Anderson.

- Be a serious-minded, mature, committed Christian with a sincere faith in Jesus Christ as Savior and Lord. Be living close to God with a clear conscience. Have the utmost trust in the power of God. Do not be skeptical of demonic activity. Fast and pray.

- Choose a location that will be free from external interference for an extended period of time.

- The counselor can work with the demonized person alone, especially using the truth encounter method, but it is good to have more than one if possible. If the counselee (demonized person) is a woman, one of the counselors should also be a woman. See Anderson (2000), p. 267.

- Make sure other possible causes for manifested symptoms have been explored.

- Make sure to lead the counselee through the necessary steps of preparation. Anderson says it is important to gather as much background information on the counselee as possible (pp. 260-61). He asks the person to fill out forms on their non-Christian spiritual experiences (pp. 202-204), and to complete a "Confidential Personal Inventory" (pp. 275-282).

- It is also important that there be general belief in sound Biblical doctrine. See Anderson, pp. 261ff.

- If you want to follow Ensign's "power encounter" method, be sure to bring a small bottle of olive oil, and some handkerchiefs or tissues, since it concludes with James 5:14ff.

II. PREPARATION FOR THE DEMONIZED PERSON

Concerning the demonized person, the first requirement is that he or she must be a Christian, an immersed believer, fully surrendered to God. James 4:7: "Submit therefore to God. Resist the devil and he will flee from you." Ed Murphy says, *"Without doubt, this surrender to God is the principal key to victory in spiritual warfare.* Ultimately, Christ's lordship is ... the pathway to breaking all demonic bondage" (*The Handbook for Spiritual Warfare*, rev. ed. [Thomas Nelson, 1997], 514-515). In the case of children (and these are sometimes demonized through adult evil), the parent(s) or guardian must be a Christian, and must go through the procedures as the child's representative (Anderson, 269-270).

Second, the counselee must be prepared to renounce and cancel all ancestral demons, i.e., all that might have been received as a child via parents' sinful or occult behavior, via Satanic Ritual abuse, or via other kinds of abuse. (Prayer may be necessary in order to help one to remember this kind of thing, says Murphy [p. 514]). This is important if the counselee is a child.

Third, the demonized person must be prepared to identify and confess all personal sins, especially major sins that can be a ground for demonic presence. (See Ephesians 4:26-27; James 5:16.) Ensign and Howe (p. 166) speak of

> ... the necessity of a thorough confession of all his major sins and especially those addictive sins which may have given grounds for Satan's control .... This confession is verbal and is before one of the elders or some other mature Christian who can give guidance in the matter. All sins of bitterness, hatred, and resentment against others in his life must be confessed and forgiveness through the blood of Jesus Christ prayed for .... Next he needs to freely forgive those who have sinned against him and ask his merciful heavenly Father to forgive them also. Among those he may have to forgive are himself and God, because he may hold an unforgiving spirit toward himself or may blame God for His failure to act as he thought He should in various matters.

This often requires much counseling, and the person must be totally honest and open. (More on this below.)

The confession is not made to everyone involved in the deliverance, but only to one person.

Finally, the counselee must be prepared to *specifically* renounce and reject all such sins and evil practices that have been confessed. These confessions and renunciations are part of the "truth encounter" advocated by Anderson, explained below. This requires sincere willingness to abandon all such sins and all related things. It includes being willing to destroy all occult objects and paraphernalia (see Acts 19:19), and includes canceling any pacts that have been made with Satan. Ensign and Howe have an example of written renunciation, which they recommend (269-270). Anderson's procedure has many such declarations and renunciations.

III. CONDUCTING THE DELIVERANCE SESSION(S)

Prayer and Scripture are of utmost importance. Prayer is crucial throughout the process. "Fervent and persistent prayer saturates our meeting with the demoniac. The burden of all the intercessions and petitions is our total dependence upon the power of the Lord Jesus Christ, giving Him all the glory and praise as He exercises His awesome power for the release of the one held captive by Satan. Complete submission to Christ and His will is repeatedly expressed and acted upon along with much praise and thanksgiving for each answer to prayer as the deliverance progresses" (Ensign and Howe, 161).

The following is a list of Bible passages that emphasize the sovereign Lordship of God and the victorious reign of Jesus Christ. They can be read aloud as needed. If a second counselor is present, he or she can read softly during the other proceedings. These texts are recommended by Ensign and Howe (p. 90, fn. 4): Psalms 18:1-19; 23; 25:1-22; 31:19-24; 32; 40:1-4; 46:1-7; 59; 69:1-15; 73:21-28; 84; 89:1-10; 91, 103; 106:1-12; 116; 118:1-18; 121; 136; 139; 145; 147; 148; 149; 150; Isaiah 40:21-31; 41:9-13; 44:24-28; 55; Jeremiah 10:6-16; 17:7-14; 32:27; Hosea 6:1-3; Micah 7:18-20; John 6:41-58; 8:31-36; 14:1-18; Romans 8; Ephesians 1:15-23; 6:10-18; Revelation 5:9-14; 11:15-18; 12:7-11; 19:1-21.

Scriptures of confession include James 5:14-18; Psalms 32; 51; Job 33:16-28. Scriptures about Christ's victory over Satan include (in addition to the above) Psalms 1; Mark 5:1-13; Philippians 2:5-11; Revelation 20:1-10.

The prayer and Scripture reading are basically preparation for the following interaction between the counselor and the counselee. Here the former leads the latter through what Anderson calls "The Seven Steps to Freedom" (pp. 199ff. in the 2000 edition of his book).

Note: a person who suspects himself or herself to be demonized may go through these steps privately in what is called self-deliverance. Also note: Anderson recommends that all prayers and declarations be stated or read ALOUD. Anderson gives copies of the prayers and declarations and renunciations to all who are present; the counselee may simply (but sincerely) read them aloud. A specific prayer and a specific declaration precede the process (p. 200).

One more note: Anderson requires anyone whom he is counseling to tell him any *negative* thoughts that come into his or her mind along the way. See pp. 264ff.

What follows now are the "Seven Steps to Freedom."

1. **Counterfeit vs. Real:** this is the verbal renunciation of "all past or present involvement with occult practices, cult teachings, and rituals, as well as non-Christian religions" (p. 201). Satan and his lies must be disavowed. Renunciation of family involvement in such practices is also important. Oral recitation of the prayers is also needed (pp. 201, 205, etc.).

2. **Deception vs. Truth:** this is the renunciation of religious and spiritual lies; renunciation of personal hypocrisy (living a lie); acceptance of the basic and fundamental truths of the Bible, especially about Jesus Christ; acceptance of the truth about oneself as being a saved, protected child of God.

3. **Bitterness vs. Forgiveness:** "The step dealing with unforgiveness is the most important one" (p. 268). In the first edition of his book Anderson said, "Most of the ground that Satan gains in the lives of Christians is due to unforgiveness" (195). Accept the hurt and the pain caused to you by others, and ask God to heal it. Specifically forgive those who have caused this pain, asking God to bring their names to your mind. "For every painful memory you have for each person on your list, pray out loud, 'Lord, I choose to forgive (name the person) for (what they did or failed to do)'" (225).

4. Rebellion vs. Submission: specifically pray for forgiveness for rebelling against God's authority and also against the various human authorities established by God (parents, government, husband, church leaders).

5. Pride vs. Humility: acknowledge areas of pride, and pray a specific prayer to live humbly before God. Allow God to show you specific areas of your life where you have been prideful.

6. Bondage vs. Freedom: this step deals with habitual sin ("sin-confess-sin-confess" etc.), and thus requires complete trust and confidentiality between the counselor and counselee. Use the help of others (James 5:16), but especially confess your sins to God. Prayerfully examine the sins of the flesh named in Mark 7:20-23, Galatians 5:19-21, and Ephesians 4:25-31. Pray that God will help you to be honest in identifying those you need to confess. Specifically renounce all sexual sin, "whether it was done to you (rape, incest, sexual molestation) or willingly by you (pornography, masturbation, sexual immorality)" (235). Anderson provides general prayers, and also special prayers for specific needs, including homosexuality, abortion, suicidal tendencies, eating disorders, self-mutilation, and substance abuse.

7. Curses vs. Blessings: "The next step to freedom is to renounce the sins of your ancestors as well as any curses which may have been placed on you." Exodus 20:4, 5 shows that "iniquities can be passed on from one generation to the next" (239-240). This generation-to-generation demonic activity shows up occasionally. Anderson said this in the first edition of this work: "Adopted children can be especially subject to demonic strongholds because of their natural parentage. But even an adopted child can become a new creation in Christ, and must actively renounce old strongholds and embrace his or her inheritance as God's child" (207).

IV. MAINTAINING THE VICTORY

Here are helpful suggestions from Anderson: "Once you have secured your freedom by going through these seven steps, you may find demonic influences attempting reentry days or even months later. One person told me that she heard a spirit say to her mind 'I'm back' two days after she had been set free. 'No, you're not,' she proclaimed aloud. The attack ceased immediately" (1990 edition, p. 208). "Even after finding freedom in Christ by going through these seven steps, you may still be attacked by demonic influences trying to regain control of your mind, hours, days, or even weeks later. But you don't have to let them. As you continue to walk in humble submission to God, you can resist the devil and he *will* flee from you (James 4:7)" (2000 edition, pp. 243-243). [Sometimes I like the old edition better!]

Other disciplines that help to preserve the victory.

1. Have an active church life.
2. Be diligent in Bible study and prayer.
3. Guard against falling back into old habits and patterns of thinking.
4. "Share your struggles openly with a trusted friend."
5. Remove all articles of false worship from your abode and pray for its cleansing.
6. Put on the whole armor of God.

DOES CASTING OUT DEMONS REQUIRE MIRACULOUS POWER?

QUESTION: Many believe that demons can still invade bodies today, and that they can be "cast out" in an act of exorcism. But does that not require supernatural power? And isn't it true that miracles have ceased? How can we explain this?

ANSWER: I believe very strongly in modern-day demonic activity, and I am very much aware of present-day "exorcisms," which occur in every area of the world. My good friend Grayson Ensign (now deceased) had a powerful and extremely beneficial deliverance ministry that began in Cincinnati; long before he died he told me that he had helped deliver over 300 people from demonic spirits.

The above question seems to assume that since all deliverance events are supernatural, those who cast out demons must have a spiritual gift from the Holy Spirit, and a *miraculous* gift at that. Thus if exorcisms still occur, then miraculous spiritual gifts must still be present. This argument is fallacious, though. The fallacy is the assumption that casting out demons is always a miraculous event. This is just not the case. We can begin by noting that "supernatural" is not the same as "miraculous." All miracles are supernatural, but not all supernatural events are miraculous.

Herein lies the difference between miracles as such, and another work of God called special divine providence, as distinct from general providence. (See my book, *What the Bible Says About God the Ruler*, for a discussion of all these works of God.) An example of special providence is answer to prayer. When we pray for God to do something in our world, and when he answers that prayer, his intervention is always supernatural but seldom miraculous. I.e., it is a work of special providence. The main difference is that in miracles, natural law is overruled; in special providence it is not. We see this distinction in God's healing of the sick. Jesus healed miraculously. Today we pray for the sick to be healed (James 5:13ff.), and God heals them providentially, in answer to our intercessory prayer.

This same distinction applies to casting out demons. This can be either miraculous, as in the case of Jesus in the Gospels; or it can be a providential answer to intercessory prayer, as in the case of the Jewish exorcists (Matthew 12:27; Acts 19:13). This is how all responsible modern-day deliverance ministers understand their work. Brother Ensign did not believe in modern-day miracles, and yet he had a very needed deliverance ministry. One should read the works of Neil T. Anderson, especially *The Bondage Breaker*, to understand deliverance as God's providential answer to intercessory prayer.

Many in deliverance ministry insist that their work does not require any special gift from the Holy Spirit; any mature Christian can do it. Robert Peterson, a missionary to Borneo who wrote *Are Demons for Real?* [emphatically, *yes*], says, "It [is] essential … to realize that all Christians of whatever race or position in the Church have equal rights before God and that God is not limited in His choice of believers to do battle with the foe. The Scriptures make it plain that the work of exorcising demons is not a special gift God has imparted to select believers, but that demons must obey any victorious Christian so long as the conditions are met. Exorcism depends on our position in Christ and not a particular gift" (p. 79).

Note also that in the four lists of spiritual gifts in the New Testament (Romans 12:1ff.; Ephesians 4:11; 1 Corinthians 12:7-11, and 1 Corinthians 12:28-30), exorcism is never mentioned.

Thus the reality of modern-day demonization, and of modern-day "exorcisms," does not contradict the view that miraculous gifts have ceased.

CAN SATAN CAST OUT DEMONS?

QUESTION: By what authority did those in Matthew 7:21-23 and Luke 9:49 apparently succeed in removing demons apart from Christ, if it is also true that "Satan cannot cast out Satan" as the Lord said in Matthew 12:26?

ANSWER: In Matthew 7:22-23 Jesus says, "Many will say to Me on that day, 'Lord, Lord, did we not prophesy in Your name, and in Your name cast out demons, and in Your name perform many miracles?' And then I will declare to them, 'I never knew you; depart from Me, you who practice lawlessness.'" From what Jesus says in v. 23, it is clear that these people are not Christians. Also, from what He does NOT say, it may be concluded that the claims of these people in v. 22 are true: they really did prophesy, do miracles, and cast out demons. I.e., He never said their claims were false. But how could they do these things if they were not Christians?

I have concluded that they do these things from the deceptive power of Satan. Satan can empower miracles (Matthew 24:24; 2 Thessalonians 2:9), even by people who *think* they are doing them in Jesus's name. All three of these activities (prophesying, which is a general term that can include tongue-speaking, Acts 2:17; working miracles, such as healing; and casting out demons) can be Satanic in origin.

But how is this consistent with what Jesus says in Matthew 12:26? In response to the Pharisees' accusation that He was casting out demons by Satan's power (v. 24), Jesus responds that this would make Satan be fighting against himself, which is self-defeating (v. 25). "If Satan casts out Satan, he is divided against himself; how then will his kingdom stand?" (v. 26). Jesus goes on to reveal that He is casting out demons by the power of the Holy Spirit (v. 28).

How may we resolve this apparent contradiction? First, the Name of Jesus in itself, representing the power and authority of Jesus, is powerful enough to force demons to leave a person, even if the one using that Name is not a true believer. That may be the case in Luke 9:49-50; see also the incident involving the seven sons of Sceva in Acts 19:13-17, where the Name of Jesus exerts power over an evil spirit in an unexpected way.

Second, there apparently were Jewish exorcists who had some success in casting out demons apart from using the Name of Jesus (Matthew 12:27; Acts 19:13). As Jews, they would be evoking the Name and power of Yahweh as He was known through Old Testament revelation. Thus it is possible that the ones of whom Jesus speaks in Matthew 7:22-23 began as Jewish exorcists and then began to use the Name of Jesus in their exorcisms without ever surrendering their lives to Christ.

There is a third consideration, however, that I believe is the best explanation of the problem here. One thing we learn, both from Scripture and from Christians who have been involved in deliverance ministry, is that there is a hierarchy of authority within the realm of demons. Satan himself is the chief demon or chief fallen angel (Matthew 12:24); he was probably an archangel before he sinned (cf. Jude 9; Revelation 12:7, where Satan seems to be equal in authority with Michael). See Mark 9:29, and Paul's frequent use of the "principalities and powers" terminology when referring to demons (e.g., Ephesians 1:21; Colossians 2:15).

What this means is that some demons are more powerful than others, and can address the weaker ones with orders that must be obeyed. For example, missionaries have testified that witch doctors possessed by powerful demons can indeed drive weaker demons out of the bodies of people who come to them for help with some kind of problem. How is this consistent with Matthew 12:26, though? The answer is provided by one of the first modern evangelical experts on demonology, Kurt Koch. He testifies that in his wide experience with occultic and demonic situations, he observed many cases where Satanic power apparently helped a victim of Satan's wiles (e.g., provided healing), but there was always a catch, or a trade-off. A Satan-follower may deliver an afflicted person from a demon that is causing one kind of problem, but the later person always develops some other kind of problem later. I can't remember Koch's exact terms here, but I think he calls this something like the "law of compensation." I.e., Satan never does something for nothing.

Thus, when Jesus suggests that Satan cannot "cast out Satan," he is referring to TRUE and complete deliverance where Satan's minions are TRULY cast out. Any situation where demons are driven out of a person by Satan's own power (as probably in Matthew 7:22) is actually a FALSE deliverance, i.e., one that is temporary or is an exchange for an even greater oppression by the devil.

"SONS OF GOD" AND "DAUGHTERS OF MEN" IN GENESIS 6:1-4

QUESTION: A member of my church has grabbed onto some strange teaching that all centers on the interpretation of Genesis 6:1-4, that the "sons of God" are fallen angels and that the "giants in the earth" (v. 4, KJV) are half human and half demonic beings basically, and that this "seed of Satan" still exists today. He weaves this together with lots of Scriptures that include in the end a certain view of biblical prophecy. Can you help?

ANSWER: Recommended resources are Merrill Unger, *Biblical Demonology*, pp. 45-52 in the edition I have; and C. Fred Dickason, *Angels: Elect and Evil*, pp. 157ff., 222-225 in my edition. I can't shed any light on the real identity of the *nephilim* (translated "giants" in the KJV), but I can say with confidence that they are NOT the offspring of fallen angels (who are identified with the "sons of God" in Genesis 6:2, 4), and human women. They may have been a human race that were exceptionally tall and large physically (similar to Goliath, 1 Samuel 17), or they may have been a cohort of exceptionally powerful kings.

The important point is the identity of the "sons of God." In the Old Testament this distinction between sons and daughters is sometimes used to refer to the good guys vs. the bad guys (e.g., Exodus 34:16; Numbers 25:1). Thus many believe that in Genesis 6:2 the writer is saying that the godly descendants of Seth (Genesis 4:25), i.e., the "sons of God," began to intermarry with the ungodly descendants of Cain, i.e., the "daughters of men." K. F. Keil and F. Delitzsch, in their classic commentary on this verse, say, "This description applies to the whole human race, and presupposes the intercourse of marriage of the Cainites with the Sethites" (*The Pentateuch*, I:127).

The idea that the "sons of God" are angelic is an old view and was found among the Jews around the time of the New Testament. A Jewish apocryphal writing called "The Book of Enoch" (some parts as early as the second century B.C.) says, "Wicked spirits came out of the body of them (i.e., of the women), for they were generated out of human beings, and from the holy watchers (angels) flows the beginning of their creation and their primal foundation. The spirits of heaven—in the heaven is their dwelling, and the spirits begotten upon earth—in the earth shall be their dwelling. And the spirits of the giants will devour, oppress, destroy, assault, do battle, and cast upon the earth and cause convulsions" (M. Unger's version of the Enoch passage, from his *Biblical Demonology*, p. 46).

I believe this view (that the "sons of God" are angelic and that they impregnated human women with continuing results) cannot be true. First, it is metaphysically impossible for angels to impregnate human women. (We should note that angels do not sexually reproduce among themselves: Matthew 22:30.) The main reason for this is that angels (fallen or unfallen) are composed of non-material spirit, and human women (for reproductive purposes) are composed of material flesh. For a woman to become pregnant, physical male sperm is necessary. Under no circumstances can angelic beings somehow turn into material stuff or be transformed into a real material body that can produce material sperm. Nor can angelic beings simply create some kind of sperm *ex nihilo*; creation *ex nihilo* is something only God can perform.

Angels can perform miracles; thus one might speculate that these "sons of God" miraculously caused pregnancies without male sperm (as in Mary's virgin conception). But the product would be wholly human, not a hybrid or combination of angel and human. Such an idea is completely unfounded, though.

A final consideration is this, that even if such unnatural beings were conceived and born (which I deny), the flood would have destroyed them all, so that none would be surviving today. Indeed, the whole purpose of the flood was to destroy the product of the marriages between "sons of God" and "daughters of men," whatever this product was. To say that such a "seed of Satan" still exists today would be to say that God's purpose for the flood failed. That is an attack on God Himself.

ABOUT THE AUTHOR*

(Photo collage – left to right/top to bottom)

1. *"The 'Pringle-Eyed Monster' tries to scare his grandchildren at a family gathering in my brother Don's condo in Sarasota, FL, around 1994. I judge the date by the presence of grandson Nick, and by the fact that the 1990 Cincinnati Reds World Series championship shirt looks fairly new. (No, the grandchildren were not scared.)"*

2. *"This is my Stamping Ground (KY) High School graduation outfit. I gave the (very brief) valedictory address for the final high school graduating class there, in the year 1955, prior to the consolidation of all the Scott County high schools the following fall. I participated in five more graduating classes (colleges and seminaries) after that, but this is the last one at which I weighed 170 pounds."*

3. Signed basketball from Indiana University (*See note #5 below.*)

4. The 1959 Cincinnati Bible Seminary graduating class. *"I am on the top row, fourth from the left. Professor Tom Friskney, in the middle, was our class sponsor. Many of my good friends from this class are still around somewhere! My greetings to you all!"*

5. Signed basketball from University of Kentucky. *"When my fulltime CCU contract was not renewed at the end of the fall 2015 semester, I taught two more courses as an adjunct professor in the spring 2016 semester. That*

---

*Photograph descriptions provided by Cathleen Cottrell with quotes from Dr. Cottrell.

was the end of my 49-year relationship with the school. Brother Lee Mason, director of the Christian Restoration Association, was rather disappointed that I was not given some kind of special recognition by the school for such a long tenure, so he decided to do that through the CRA. Thus, part of the fall 2016 CRA Bible Conference banquet (in Mason, OH) was a very nice program honoring me for that service to Christ's kingdom. (Thank you, Lee! Thank you, CRA!)

In addition to a very nice love gift from the CRA trustees and banquet attendees, I was given two special gifts. The first was dear to the heart of this lifelong University of Kentucky basketball fan: a UK basketball signed by coach John Calipari (lower left)! Not to be outdone, some Indiana University supporter heard this was going to happen, so he secured an IU basketball signed by coach Tom Crean (whoever that is; top right). Being the nice person that I am, I tried to accept the second one with as much grace as I possibly could."

6. *"I'm sitting at the teacher's table in a CBS classroom early in my full-time teaching career there, which began in the fall of 1967. I know the student looks as if he is listening to his cell phone, but that was a bit too early for that kind of distraction. He is probably just dozing."*

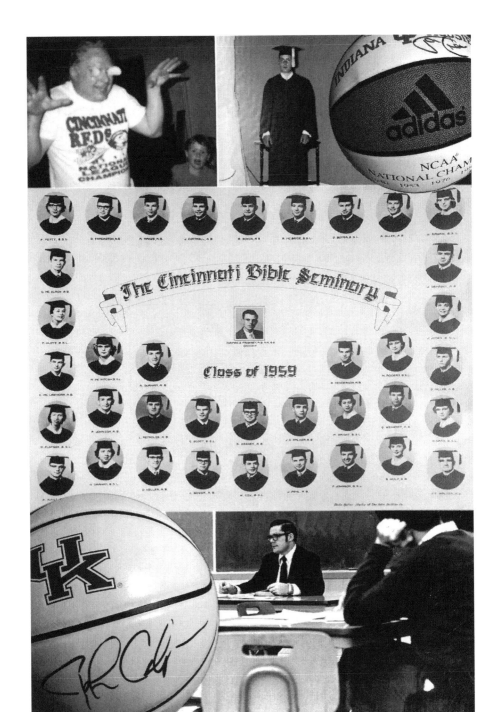

The Collected Writings of Jack Cottrell

Proudly made available by
The Christian Restoration Association
www.theCRA.org

Made in the USA
Columbia, SC
31 December 2022

75242493R00124